Presented To:

_____

From:

_____

Date:

_____

Message:

_____

_____

_____

_____

_____

_____

THE GOLDEN
GOOSE
BECOMES AN
AUTHORPRENEUR

Proven Hacks to Self-Publishing Within a Year

By Grant Senzani

Figure 1 The Five Pillars of Self-Publishing ©

Copyright and Credits © 2020 Grant Senzani

ISBN: 978-0-620-84791-9 (Print)
ISBN: 978-0-620-88061-9 (eBook)

Illustrator: Motsanaphe Morare (MoMaLifeLiving.com)
Illustrator: Siwe Mfeka

Editor and Proof-reader: Sonia Soneni Dube
(sdube@thegoldengooseinstitute.com)

The Golden Goose Series©

I would love to hear from you. Your questions, your comments are welcome. Don't be a stranger. My contact information is listed below, and I encourage you to contact me in whatever way is easiest for you. I am also available for speaking engagements.

My email address is info@thegoldengooseinstitute.com

This book was published by The Golden Goose Institute (Pty) Ltd

For further information email: info@thegoldengooseinstitute.com

DEDICATION

To You the Aspiring Author,

As you page through this book you will realize
that writing and publishing

a book is not a farfetched dream.

Matter of fact, you always had it within you.

All I am doing is telling you it is possible and
pushing you off the ledge of procrastination into
the ocean depth of your dreams.

Stop procrastinating!

Read this, then write and publish your book!

The world is waiting and so am I.

Love,

Grant

ACKNOWLEDGEMENTS

To Anna Ngarachu,

Your unconditional love and consistent reminders that I can do and become better have

become evident in who I am becoming.

Thank you. Don't stop.

To Luyanda Dlamini,

My first client.

Words fall short at the faith you had in my talent to help you become an author

while I was yet to articulate my offering.

May success perpetually follow you in all your endeavors and

may your clients be just as supportive.

Thank you.

To Dad, Mum, Aubrey, and Khangeziwe,

We have a beautiful family and I have no doubt

as to how that has affected my desire to want and become more.

Thank you all for that.

FOREWORD

Grant Senzani provides an exceptional asset for any writer to have in their list of resources. It begins by asking the reader (future author) to imagine the details of their book launch. This allows the future author to bring that eventual event to the fore and feel the emotions of reaching the mountain top. He then leads the future author through the path of getting to that mountain top.

This book was written from experiences gained through publishing *When the Golden Goose Doesn't Lay Eggs – Lessons on Fulfilling Your Potential*. This was Grant's first offering which then sparked the creation of the Golden Goose book series, The Golden Goose Institute, book writing workshops, and eventually a publishing house. Grant has demonstrated the importance of having a dream and having the tenacity to follow through on achieving it.

He has broken down the daunting task of publishing a book into manageable chunks of sub-tasks which make the attainment of the goal seem more possible. He has shown the relative ease of getting a book published within a year through implementing a system.

Reading the book is not just a matter of understanding the journey that Grant went through to publish his book, but is an active guide to help you as you start your journey. The system works only if you put in the effort to follow it. I would encourage you to make it practical as opposed to theoretical.

If you are experiencing reservations about publishing your book - being concerned about which people would buy a book from someone relatively unknown - I can assure you that you are not alone. We go through those fears of not being good enough or capable of sharing our work with others, but we publish anyway. You have a story to tell as you have been blessed to experience life through your eyes. Your message may be a gift that changes a life. Do not deny the world that gift.

I am honored to have been the first client to go through the process from idea to published book in less than a year. I had my struggles during the process as my life took an unexpected turn. Even with that detour, I managed to complete what I had started through the coaching provided by Grant. It really is possible to get this done. Just start.

Thank you, Grant, for compiling this book and sharing your authentic stories and the lessons you learned along the way. It is a gem that will enhance the lives of many aspiring authors to get from aspiring to accomplished.

DTM Luyanda Dlamini M.M.
– Entrepreneur and Author of "What Had Happened Was...: How to Build Inner Strength When Your World Crumbles"

HOUSE RULES

Just as a matter of house rules, if this is the first book you are purchasing from me then I need to fill you in on what you have missed out on.

My first book was entitled ***When the Golden Goose doesn't Lay Eggs: Lessons on Fulfilling Your Potential***. It's predicated on the fact that we are all filled with potential and this is what makes us golden. We, however, do not always reach our full potential. The book answers why we don't reach our full potential and how we could start doing so.

This book in your hands is the extension of that idea. You have the potential to write and publish a book; here is why you haven't, and here is how you could. Readers of this book will learn how to write and publish a quality book within a year.

Subsequently, my company "The Golden Goose Institute", with strategic business partners, was birthed from these series. If you see the words "our company" this is what I am referring to. Our company at the sole is a publisher that creates and teaches authors how to create a business from their literary work. The book I first authored allowed me to walk into doors and charge fees I would have never been able to without it. A book to me is a business first, but more on that later.

Lastly, if you haven't guessed it yet the word "Authorpreneur" is a mixture of two words: author and entrepreneur. It is an author that builds a business from their book.

Right, I have held your attention long enough. Flip the page and let's get you started on your journey.

PREFACE

Can I ask you to do yourself a huge favor? For this book to make any sense to you, I want you to take a moment to use your imagination: I want you to imagine your book launch. Would it be held during the weekend, or maybe during the week? What time of day would be best?

Wait, but that is not all I want you to imagine. I want you to imagine more. I want the details. Tell me the theme of your book launch. What are you wearing? Did you invite guest speakers? What foods do you have displayed for your guests? How many people are in attendance? How do you feel about how well everything is going; from the insightful moments to the fun and laughter? Lastly, the standing ovation you received; what emotions were running through you in that moment as people got up to their feet to celebrate you?

Take a moment to answer those questions intentionally even if it is briefly.

What you have just imagined has happened in the most important place. It has happened in your mind - the birthplace of all reality. Whether you know it or not this imagination has triggered an unending need to be realized. So, dear aspiring author, how do you make this imagination transform into reality?

As you ponder on the answer, allow for me, in no less than 35,000 words, to share with you how I did and how others in your shoes have done the same thing. Feel free to take what you feel will guide you into making that quantum leap from aspiring to accomplished author and discard the rest either completely or for another time entirely.

My guidance is predicated by the workshops we as a company have run and the aspiring authors, we have helped become published. I want to blatantly admit to you that my guidance will not serve you as answers, only you can come up with that. My guidance is here to shed the light on what you already know the answer to be. That you are an author, you always were. It is just a matter of time until the whole world catches on.

Let's get the world to catch on.

OTHER BOOKS
BY GRANT SENZANI

When the Golden Goose Doesn't Lay Eggs
Lessons on Fulfilling Your Potential

The Golden Goose Learns How to Master Selling
Proven Methods that will Grow Your Sales Exponentially

CONTENTS

The Golden Goose Becomes An Authorpreneur

INTRODUCTION

In my experience, any aspiring author faces 5 problems before they begin to put their pen to a page in order to start expressing their ideas. The problems are as follows:

1. Lack of structure for their content.
2. Lack of pragmatic goal setting techniques to start and finish their book.
3. Lack of proper research.
4. Lack of an entrepreneurial spirit.
5. Lack of marketing.

1. Lack of structure for your content

The first and most important component in writing a book is structure. Chances are that you already have the information on hand, but it's not about the information as much as it is how the information is communicated. Your reader is meant to flip from page to page, read from the front all the way to the back cover, and then walk away with something implementable.

Having what I have coined a "Golden Thread" will ensure your reader will go through your book and not have a blank look when they are done reading it. Instead, they will rant and rave about it, and then refer it to friends.

2. Lack of pragmatic goal setting techniques

Your book will not write itself. You have to put those words down until they compose a book.

For some this takes years; personally, I believe you could achieve this easily within a year. I have taught individuals and groups on how to get to their goals faster than they had anticipated. You can too if you have the right goal setting techniques and could publish your book much sooner without compromising on quality either.

3. Lack of proper research

Your opinions and facts are valid. What would ensure your reading audience buying into them even more is when there has been extensive research done. We may not admit it as individuals but social proofing - what other people think of you and your work - is important, and therefore it is paramount to share what other experts think of your findings. This book will show you how to research without drowning, dampening, or diluting your voice in your message.

4. Lack of an entrepreneurial spirit

Great, so you finally have a book, but if your book has really solved a problem then you will have a plethora of opportunities that need to be actualized. It may be seminars, workshops, speaking engagements, or even consulting.

The mistake I made with my first book was that I did not think this issue through completely. You can learn from me and will do better than I did. I have faith in you.

I will give you a synopsis of how you could do this because let's face it; while book sales are great, you will not make as much money in book sales as you can in leveraging your book for larger paying opportunities.

5. Lack of marketing

In workshops we have hosted as a company, I have had stories of people that have a garage of their book gathering dust and being eaten by moths.

From the onset, you need to be marketing before your book comes out, when it does come out, and after it has come out too. This is a never-ending process and as long as you spend at least 15-20 minutes per day looking for means and ways to market, then you are well on your way to ensuring there is room in your garage for your book to fill, temporarily.

I have dedicated the last section of this book to just marketing so that your book perpetually flies from your garage into the homes of the readers it is intended for.

So, what's next?

Sit back, relax, grab a pen, and open your notebook. You are about to turn your book idea from potential into results.

LACK OF STRUCTURE – HOW TO CREATE THE GOLDEN THREAD

"Without a solid foundation you'll have trouble creating anything of value" – Unknown

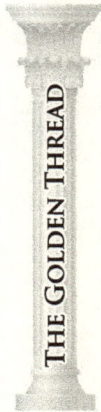

THE GOLDEN THREAD

Figure 2 The Five Pillars of Self-Publishing © - The Golden Thread

CHAPTER 1
FOUNDATION?

There is a famous story told of two builders[1]. These two builders wanted to build astonishing homes. Both were fully capable of building these astonishing places of habitation; the only difference that these two homes had was the foundation which they built on.

You are about to write a book. You may get your marketing right; you may have the best of book covers and the most prolific people reviewing your book, but it is only when your reader finishes your book that you will know whether you really had something to share or it was all just smoke and mirrors.

More on that soon, let's get back to the story.

Why foundations matter...

While it was sunny and the weather was great, both homes looked worthwhile for occupation.

---

1   The Holy Bible, Luke 6:46 - 49

They both looked astonishing from the outside. The only thing that separated them was one was built close to the seashore, while the other was built on a cliff made of solid rock overlooking the sea.

One day, a storm broke out. The sea level began to rise. The rains fell down harshly and the winds blew wildly. Both of these home's structures were severely tested. This lasted for a whole night, but I am sure if you were in any of those homes it would have felt like an eternity.

The morning after, the winds had disappeared and the rain was gone. All that remained were the two homes that had been violently visited. Can guess which house remained intact?

As you begin to piece your book together, you have a unique choice: you get to pick which builder you are in this story. Your first choice is to spew word for word until you finally have a book because essentially that is what a book is; a compilation of words. Your second option, however, would be you going the extra mile and ensuring every word is carefully orchestrated and is building towards a specific objective.

Whatever your choice, your book will be tested once it meets with the eyes of your reader. From cover to cover your reader will break your ideas down to make the most sense of them. Remember, readers read to learn and augment their reality with the help of your insight.

If there is no flow, if there is no structure to your book, you will end up with a disgruntled reader. That disgruntled reader, through word of mouth, will spread their experience of your book and that may prove detrimental to your book's sales.

One of my goals currently is to read 1000 books. I started this goal on the 1st of January 2018; as of the 30th of March 2020, I have read 185 books. I can tell you from experience that flow and structure count. The better yours are, the higher the potential of your reader's engagement.

This structure and flow I have aptly coined the "Golden Thread". Your book will either rise or fall because of the quality of its Golden Thread.

The books that have gripped my imagination and have forced me to think and act differently have always been the ones with a strong Golden Thread. They are also the books I have recommended and sometimes forced my friends to buy as well. I have seen how Golden Threads are made and now I will show you how you can create one for your work of art. It is something I teach at our company's workshops and in our one-on-one author coaching sessions.

The proof in the pudding though is when my clients come back with reviews from their readers. Often their readers mention to them how coherent their books were, how easy they were to follow, and how easy they will be to implement. As a result, the author and I - whether over Skype, Zoom, email, or a phone call - share a smile of a noteworthy achievement.

> **QUICK QUESTION:**
> Do you have a Golden Thread?

Before I show you how to develop a Golden Thread, let me further share with you the importance of developing one.

CHAPTER 2
THE IMPORTANCE OF A GOLDEN THREAD

It's not about you...

At the end of the day, everything you write is not meant for you. It is meant for your reader. Your reader comes first. It is important to remember this because some of the books I have read have the author's bravado displayed from cover to cover and leave no value behind for their reader. Books are made for readers, not for the author.

Books that are written from the basis of bravado without consideration for the reader will inevitably end up staying with the author. Leave your bravado behind. Learn to put your reader first. The Golden Thread teaches you how to do that succinctly.

Another reason you should consider having a Golden Thread is congruence.

Congruence

The first book I wrote was all over the place when it came to what I was writing about. It was well written as a sum but in thought, there were disparities. What did this look like?

Someone would admit that I was a good writer and then would confess that they didn't get how some chapters tied in with the others.

A Golden Thread allows you to have all your chapters congruent and heavily centered around a theme. That theme will ensure that every word, sentence, paragraph, chapter, and page will add more meat to your thoughts as an author. This will enable your reader to follow through with you every step of the way without missing a beat.

Building a business

Remember, you are going to do plenty more with your book apart from just sell it. You are going to leverage it to get speaking engagements or start workshops, courses, coaching sessions, or seminars. Your Golden Thread will allow you to build all of these with a rich amount of purpose and executable objectives.

It will also spur your mind to look for possible opportunities your book could open you up to and what products or services will allow you to optimize those opportunities.

Marketing

A Golden Thread will allow you to build great marketing messages for your target audience. This message will drive past their minds and land on their hearts because you will be speaking directly to them.

Would you like an audience that is drawn to you? Then master your Golden Thread.

Avoiding the dreaded "Writers Block"

A Golden Thread circumvents writer's block. The more pronounced your Golden Thread is, the easier it is to write. As I am writing this book, I have divided my screen into two. On the right side of the screen is the word document of this book. On the left side is the mind map of the book that I completed on a free software called Freemind.

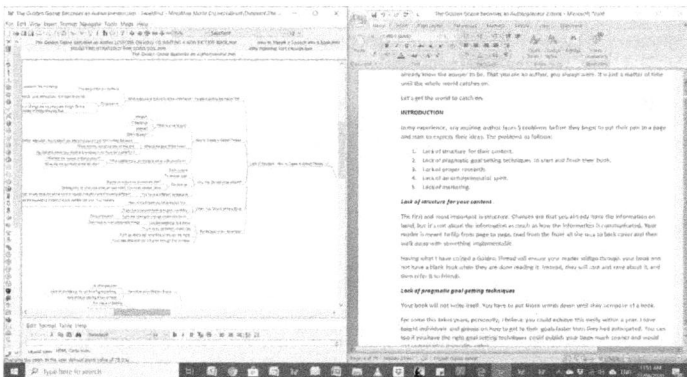

Figure 3 Example of Freemind

Each time I briefly look at my ideas, whether I am beginning to write or taking a break between writing; my words start to flow and that flow keeps going. The opposite of this flow is staring at a blank screen while twiddling your thumbs in hopes that the words that will fill your page will eventually come to you. In effect, this is like a car revving while the gearbox is still in neutral. The intention to move may be there but the car remains stagnant. Intention never delivers results but action always will.

The Golden Thread will allow for that.

Improved goal setting

A Golden Thread ensures that you begin to see how long your book will take to publish. The more your Golden Thread is fleshed out, the longer it will take write out.

Would you like to know how long your book will take to write? Develop a Golden Thread.

Research anyone?

Let's face it, you and I know a lot of things but we do not know everything. This also applies to experts in any field. No one knows everything. A Golden Thread allows you to have your thoughts all mapped out. The more mapped out your thoughts are, the more you can take into cognizance what would be missing from your book and then add it if necessary.

Therefore, the Golden Thread of your book allows for better research.

Is it worth it?

The last thing your Golden Thread will reveal to you is whether it will be worthwhile to actually write and publish your book.

If you are thinking of self-publishing, then you have to realize that you may run a loss. Your Golden Thread will reveal this to you upfront, which will, in turn, save you time and money.

I know it might not be the popular thing to say but if your book will leave you worse off than where you are right now then perhaps looking at other avenues to express your thoughts would be a better alternative. You could try blogging or submitting magazine articles on your subject matter.

I want you and your book to win, so it is my duty to share both sides of the coin with you. Ultimately if you rely on a strong Golden Thread, you will do fine.

> **QUICK QUESTION:**
> What is the importance of a Golden Thread?

Now you know the importance of a Golden Thread. Let's address how you create one.

CHAPTER 3
HOW TO BUILD A
GOLDEN THREAD

Like the builder who built on a solid foundation, it will take you long to put this together. I would easily recommend a month although, in a one-on-one session with either with my team members or me, we could get you to formulate your Golden Thread in less than 2 hours. This is due to the prepared and sequenced questions we have collated for you before-hand. Whether on your own or with our aid, the Golden Thread will show its value throughout the lifetime of your book.

Shall we begin?

Great, tell me what is the goal of your book?

Step 1: What's your book's goal?

Understand, acknowledge, and articulate what your book will do for you once it is published and circulating in the world. What benefit will that have for you? Will you now be recognized as an authority in your industry? Are you looking to make another income stream? Are you trying to change career paths? Or is it just a dream of yours that you would like to fulfil?

Knowing the goal of your book will ensure that you understand whether or not your book is a success or failure.

My first book's goal was fuzzy and not completely outlined. Only after publishing it did I mention what I wanted from the book. As you would have guessed by then it was too late.

The goal for your book also determines how your book will be written from the onset and to whom it will be targeted as well.

With my first book, I wanted to have speaking engagements and to create a secondary income. Had that been articulated from the onset, what would have emerged would have been writing geared towards the goal; letting the reader know that I am a phenomenal speaker and that I would like the opportunity to speak. This clear intention would have then allowed the reader to take notice and if the reader loved the book, the outcome of a speaking engagement would be very likely. I have seen this personally through the books I have read and the authors I have related with.

If you do know what your book will do for you then I would like for you to write it out now completely. Yes, stop this moment and write it out in full.

....
....
....
....
....
....
....

Contrary to what I mentioned at the beginning of this book, this is the only time you get to think of yourself and what you need out of this process. After the setting of your goal, everything becomes about the reader.

QUICK QUESTION:
What is the goal of your book?

Now that you have your goal it's time to look at the book through your reader's eyes. How you begin to address this is by asking yourself the question, "What problem does my book solve?"

Writing out the goal of your book was step one, step two is about solving a problem. Flip the page to figure out what problem your book will solve.

CHAPTER 4
HEY SHERLOCK

Every book published solves a problem, whether fiction or non-fiction. Some books are overt with the problem they are trying to solve, others aren't but they are still built with that thought in mind.

If your book does not solve a problem then it would not be wise to write the book until you have figured that out.

You do this by figuring out the answer to the question, "Once my reader is done with my book, they will improve _____ with their lives."

You then take that _____ and put it as a specific negative. So, if your book is about your reader improving their finances perhaps, you would then narrow in on what they would improve on financially. Is it saving? Investing? Debt management? Cash flow management?

The more specific the problem you would like to address the easier it will be to write about it and have solid solutions for it as well.

Have you written it out?

Step 2: Causes

The second step would be to write out in a list format what the causes of that problem are. Have at least 10 causes. The first 5 will be easy to come up with, the 6th and 7th will take you some time and the 8th, 9th, and 10th will have you scratching your head.

Nonetheless, I want you to list these. The point of this exercise is to figure out what you know and what you may be missing as well. This is how you also begin to develop into an expert or realize that you are one. If you do not know the causes of the problem you wish to solve then this is your first point of call to begin researching.

Step 3: Solutions, please?!

Every book needs a problem, the causes of that problem, and then the solutions to those causes. The solutions stem from how the cause became a cause and what your solutions are to that cause.

An exercise we give out at this specific point is that for every cause (at least 10) that you have listed, you need to find 4-5 solutions to that cause. This will be tiring. I have seen how by the time our clients get to the 3rd problem, they are looking at us with puppy eyes and asking for mercy. Our response? "Only when you are done".

After the exercise, although drained, most clients will undoubtedly remark, "Wow, thank you! This has been very insightful. I highly appreciate it!" After you have gone through the torture, I know you will too.

At this point, you have outlined your problem, the causes of your problem, and the solutions to them as well. These actions are what form the bedrock to the content of your book. Let me show you how.

Treat the Golden Thread of your book as the roots of a tree. The trunk is the problem that you are going to solve, the branches (chapters) the causes, and the leaves are the solutions (sub-chapters). The fruits of your tree are the ad hoc products and services that you will create; but more of that at a later stage of the book.

> **QUICK QUESTION:**
> What are the solutions to the causes of the problem that you are solving?

I am sure that by now you are slowly seeing the magic begin to happen. Your book's foundation is beginning to form in a phenomenal fashion.

They are two more steps to finishing this process, however. These steps are to write down the promise you make to the reader and how that will be communicated to them.

Wait, what promise did I make to the reader?

Before you think, "Oh, more work?", relax. Remember the problem you wrote out? Well, that problem is written out in a negative way. The promise you are going to develop expresses the problem in a way that shows it has now been solved.

This is what your reader will walk away with.

In the case of this book, the problem I wish to solve is: "Why people take so long to write and publish books and why certain books lack the depth to augment the reality of the reader."

The promise would then read as: "Readers of this book will learn how to write and publish a quality book within a year." This is also how a subtitle is formed. You are welcome.

You are not done yet, because you have to know how you will communicate this promise to the reader.

To complete that promise, you will have to know whether you are looking to entertain, inspire, persuade, or inform.

How can you communicate your promise?

You express your promise through 4 ways.

You either:

1. Entertain
2. Inspire
3. Persuade
4. Inform

Let me expand on these.

1. Entertaining

Entertaining is about intentionally altering the emotional state of your reader. You do this by storytelling, which is the best way to engage your reader's emotions whether it is joy, laughter, or sadness. If you are a natural storyteller then this will be relatively easy for you. If, however, you are like me and you like facts and figures, with tables and charts, then this is something that you will have to learn to do. I would advise joining a Toastmasters club where you would learn the art of storytelling. You could also read a book on how to build a story or read books with compelling stories. Once you have done your homework, then I'd want you to write a story and give it to someone to read. After they are done reading, ask to see what they felt. Be sure to only ask after they have read so as not to pre-empt them to think or respond in a manner that would validate your work.

I also want you to know that not all stories are created equal. If you had to see this from a hierarchical point of view then the most engaging stories will be about yourself, followed by those about other people, and then fictional stories. As you tell stories in your book, keep that in mind.

This doesn't mean you then focus on yourself; it is just to bring you awareness.

2. Inspiring

You could also inspire your reader. This entails understanding how to get someone to move from their current ideals to a higher ideal. Spiritual material such as the Bible or the Qur'an do this very well. Some autobiographies also do this very well such as "A Man's Search for Meaning" by Viktor Frankl. These books seek to better your character, for you to live a noble and moral life with greater self-awareness of the higher ideals you can obtain. They also teach you why you should obtain such in life and how as well. These are also heavy with storytelling because most of us are naturally attracted to stories more than facts, figures, lists, charts, or graphs.

Inspiring work allows us to resonate with the characters of a story and through those character's mistakes and victories, we learn how to achieve the same results using them as an example.

To really inspire your reader, obtain real stories and if possible, stories of your own. These have a better pull on your reader's emotions and will also ensure that your inspiration can be achieved pragmatically by the reader.

3. Persuading

The third is persuading. Persuasion in the context of communication has the sole purpose of getting the reader to support and transform their thinking in favor of the presenter's perspective[2]. How you persuade and what the difference is between persuasion and inspiration is pretty simple. You persuade by comparing your proposition with the current proposition of the reader. You then show the reader why it would be more beneficial to ride on your bandwagon as opposed to staying on theirs. The difference between persuasion and inspiration is that persuasion is mainly linear thinking e.g. why you should consider one car as opposed to another. Inspiration, however, is nonlinear e.g. why drive when you can teleport?

While storytelling is important in persuading your reader's thoughts from theirs to yours, it needs to be backed by information that will validate them discarding their current notion. The reason for your stories is to emotionally connect with your reader. The empirical data is to ensure that they stick to the new thoughts you may want them to buy into. If this resonates with you, ensure your stories are very intentional and include empirical data to prove their validity.

---

2   https://www.quora.com/What-is-persuasive-communication

4. Informing

The last way to express your ideas is by informing. This is merely the sharing of facts or essential information. Textbooks are at the top of the list for this. From my experience in reading, authors such as Robert Greene and his mentee Ryan Holiday do a great job of this. They are informers. They give you the facts and support them with factual stories from history. These books for me are the easiest to buy into because I can always research the information shared. They are however very academic-like and can sometimes feel like an information overload.

Out of the 4 of these, you should pick one primary expression for your Golden Thread but if you are tempted to pick more, ensure it does not surpass two. Any more than two and you will have to assess what outcome you truly desire.

As a publishing company, we offer DISC assessments to all our clients. What these assessments do is map out how you naturally communicate. This enlightens the writer as to how they would be perceived from a reader's point of view. Therefore, from the onset, they already know whether they are entertaining, inspirational, persuasive, or informative writers. If they choose to challenge themselves by not writing in line with their behavior types, one of our consultants shows them how to do this.

In my case, the promise of this book is: To inform and persuade aspiring authors to write and self-publish a quality book within a year. Also, note that according to my DISC assessment this ties in hand in hand with how I naturally communicate.

QUICK QUESTION:
What promise does your book fulfil?

At this point, you should have your Golden Thread mapped out. The next chapter highlights what you ought to write about and how to do it.

CHAPTER 5
WHAT DO I WRITE ABOUT?

I know there are two types of aspiring authors that are paging through this book. The first know what they want to write about, the second don't, and are still trying to figure it out. I would like to dedicate the next portion specifically to those that don't know what to write about. If you do know what you want to write about, you can skip to the next subtitle.

But Grant, what should I write about?

The ideas that follow I got from Hassan Osman's *'Write Your Book on the Side How to Write and Publish Your First Nonfiction Kindle Book While Working a Full-Time Job'*[3] I'll simply iterate them and add my own spin on how I am using them in my work.

---

3   https://www.amazon.com/Write-Your-Book-Side-Nonfiction-ebook/dp/B01MY6YT2P

Essentially, Hassan makes the point that what you write about should consider 4 things. The 4th, however, is optional:

Experience

You should write about something that you have experienced and that you feel is noteworthy to share. Experience ensures the reader that you are not sucking things out of your thumb. It highlights how you know what you are talking about. This results in building rapport with your reader and also decreases the number of objections your reader will have throughout your book.

There is also a level of authenticity that you express when you speak from experience. I personally buy books for this reason. Even though most books are similar when it comes to the message shared and expressed, what really differentiates them from one another are the personal experiences expressed. Ultimately, we all want to take advice from people who have already walked the journey as opposed to those that have the theory about it.

I was watching a documentary on veteran soldiers who watch war movies. The feedback from most of them was that they were turned off by how the actors use artillery. They could tell that the actors did not know what they were doing. As with you, if you are speaking about what you have not experienced someone will pick it out. I would advise that you avoid this and the drama that could ensue as a result of it. If you must share something you have not experienced, however, then ensure that insight is based on someone else's story that has experienced what you would like to share.

I once read a book about what makes billionaires because this is one of my pursuits. I felt something was off as I read it. Prompted by my feelings I did a Google search on the author. Guess what? The author was not a billionaire. I still cry over this to this day. Feel free to send me tissue if your heart is moved to.

Experience is essential, but so is the next step.

Interest

In sales we are taught that if we do not believe in our products or services, it will show up in the enthusiasm we express as we pitch it to prospects in the hope that they will buy from us.

The interest in your book from any reader should never surpass that of your own. The reader should feel with every word how passionate you are about your subject matter. If the reader picks up your lack of interest, which we do, it will only mean one less customer in the long run. This affects both your revenue and more importantly the fact that you could not help that customer any further.

So, whatever you write about has to be something you are interested in and that interest must be translated into your writing.

The other benefit of writing about your interest is that it will allow your customer to transfer that energy to their friends or family by recommending your book to their circles. Needless to say, this is how a book begins to fly off your shelf or out of the boot of your car into the homes and offices of your customers.

The third essential step is to understand whether there is a market for your book. Well is there?

Where is the market?

Is there a market for the topic you have experience with?

A very easy way to find this out is to ask around and look at Amazon when you get the chance to as well. This will let you know whether investing your time and money into writing your book will be worthwhile.

The market is really a fancy way of saying "a large body of interested buyers". These buyers will ensure that your book translates into income. If people are not willing to buy or have not bought a book like the one you are looking to release, perhaps going back to the drawing board would be best. You deserve to win in the market place, and I want you to. Don't make a loss in time or money; find out what the market wants of which you are both interested and have experience with. This will translate into a win for you and a win for your audience.

You may argue the point that you would like to be a pioneer. I for one love such a venturous soul. Take into account both the fact that while you could win, there is a chance of failure too. So, whether you take the plunge or not, do so on the grounds of being honest with yourself. This is not to prevent you from writing your book. This is me asking you to do so with caution.

How I found my market for this book was when I would keep being asked: "Can you teach me how to write a book?" It was not something I had anticipated. Subsequently from receiving all this interest, I then developed an author workshop entitled *'How to Write and Self Publish Your Book in a Year'*.

After the first workshop, the rest have been sold out. This further validated how writing a book would ensure I make the most of the opportunity granted to me. My story does not need to be different from yours. I am like you and the only difference is the process that I followed. I want you to win. I want this to be you. I can never express my need for you to win enough, so expect me to keep telling you.

The last thing you can write about is something work-related and this is optional.

Work-related?

This is the only part that is negotiable for you as an aspiring author. You do not need to write about your profession. The difference between this and experience is that I could be a doctor as a profession but have experience in public speaking and want to write about public speaking.

While it is certainly negotiable, I will advise that writing on your profession will give you the stamp of credibility and authority in your industry. Using this and leveraging it with your interest, experience, and a willingness to buy the audience could prove to be more profitable.

'*Could*' is the magic word because you may lock yourself in a specific niche that you could lose relevance in if there is no more new material to share or your niche seizes to be relevant. So, ensure you have this in the back of your mind if you decide to write about your profession.

You should by now have a great idea of what to write on. I will now propose to you why you should write. You may think, "But Grant, I would have not bought this book if I did not have the thought in mind or if I didn't want to write." You may feel this way now, but when you begin to write, I promise your emotions will want to betray you. Here is how you will combat them.

> **QUICK QUESTION:**
> Do you know what you would like to write about?

Knowing what your book should be about is important. Along the journey of your writing, you will have to encourage yourself with why you ought to write a book or complete the one you are currently writing. The next chapter deals with that.

CHAPTER 6
WHY SHOULD I WRITE A BOOK?

There are thousands of reasons why you should write a book. I won't keep you hostage to this book for that long. Instead, I would like you to consider four reasons carefully:

1. To develop a new income stream
2. To transform lives
3. To build your confidence
4. To start a new career

To develop a new income stream

I don't know about you but the more I listen to financial gurus, the more I begin to realize that you cannot live off of one income stream for two main reasons. The first is that if you are only dependent on one income stream then what happens when that dries up?

This I learned from my loving and hardworking father. He had a job that paid benefits that allowed our family to travel the whole of Southern Africa while schooling at the top schools in each of those countries. Needless to say, the homes we lived in were immaculate only being outdone by our diplomat friends.

Once my dad lost his job, it felt as though we began a new life at negative zero. The school I went to thereafter was the first school where there were only people of my race. Usually, I was the minority.

During his time of unemployment, my father became entrepreneurial and started a company. "Lakeland Explorations" he called it; till today that still has a ring to my heart. This ordeal, however, has permanently reminded me how you cannot be dependent on one source of income. I have even gone as far as ensuring the beautiful and highly intelligent lady I am engaged to feels the same way and is en route to creating a secondary income of her own.

Look, what happened to my dad was unfortunate, but how he came out of it has changed my outlook and inspired me to search for more sources of income. It is therefore with heartfelt gratitude that I say, "Thank you Dad, for being exemplary."

Now you may say, "Grant, I will just use my money wisely and become a minimalist." Do you believe you were put on this earth to cower and settle for the meager crumbs on the floor when there is a banquet on the table?

I challenge you to live a life of abundance. You could do so by labeling some jars the following:

1. The going out fund,
2. The holiday fund,
3. The new clothes fund,
4. The charity fund,
5. The children's tertiary fund or
6. The traveling fund.

Then think about how your book sales and the opportunities they grant you could grow those funds further.

Eric Thomas & Associates have a podcast I religiously listen to every Friday. It's hosted by CJ Quinney, with co-hosts Eric Thomas and Karl Philips. On their 163rd episode – The 9 to 5 Millionaire[4] - they interviewed Jamal King who has now become an additional member of the podcast.

Jamal King, a police officer at the time of the recording, was already a millionaire. His millions were generated from owning various real estate and businesses.

---

4   https://www.youtube.com/watch?v=vgKkUusGg-o

His premise for generating more income came from wanting to service every bill he had with income either from a property or from business revenue. I am not a millionaire yet, but his principle is sound and should be looked at and acted upon seriously. To date, I have more income streams generated from my first book, and with this second one I will now do the same.

The sales of your book may not grant you the largest of luxuries upfront but it will open the door, in the long run, to ensure you earn more. The money you generate could pay for expenses or luxuries.

Pay the price, write your book, and let time reward you for your efforts financially.

Lastly, nothing makes me happier than when I know my clients now have another income and I was able to help them with that. It really gives me a funds feeling of fulfilment. I have had clients who just through book sales are able to pay a couple of their mortgage payments. That is quite the achievement.

It's time you transformed a life!

Did you know that you have the ability to change lives? Do you know there is a story within you? Your unique perspective can and will alter someone's life if you find the bravery to write and publish it.

You may argue, "Grant, I get you and that sounds positive! Do you understand the number of books that are published yearly? Do you understand that I am merely a droplet in an ocean of knowledge?" To which I respond, "Yes! I know that much is true but I also know that regardless of the ocean of knowledge, you have a unique perspective. You have a unique story and body of knowledge, and perhaps you ought to stop looking at it from a comparison point of view and instead begin to see your story as you should. Your story is its own ocean. It is not a droplet. It never was."

After my first book, *When the Golden Goose doesn't Lay Eggs: Lessons on Fulfilling Your Potential* [5]came out, I went through the same nerves that you did. I thought to myself, "Grant, what qualifies you, and what makes you think you have something to share?" My need to write my book, however, would challenge that notion time and time again. Upon releasing my book, I had people writing back to me, letting me know how the book had affected them positively. They would share how they enjoyed the stories and the humor-infused principles that I shared. I didn't see that at the beginning of my journey. It only unfolded once

---

5   https://www.amazon.com/dp/B075THJXZN

I released my book. The same goes for you. You may not see the change now, but you will once you publish your book.

An extra scoop of confidence anyone?

I have at times walked into my friends' homes and looked at their bookshelves or mini-libraries. I love books and so before I see how huge their TVs are, the bookshelves are the sacred place that my eyes are drawn to first. When I see my book on their shelf my heart leaps with joy. I may not always show it but it does add a brick to my wall of confidence as it will for you too.

It validates that my ideas mean something and are worth sharing.

It's also flattering to know that once upon a time that book on their shelf was an idea. It reminds me of how powerful we are as humans. How we can work on an idea until it's a realization.

What's more, is the fact that they paid for my book as well. Can you believe it? My idea is worth someone else's hard-earned finances. Let that sink in as you are up next.

If you are struggling with confidence, then this is certainly something you ought to do. It will build it.

If you are not struggling with confidence, then this is a way to build it further because confidence is a muscle and in order to grow a muscle, you must exercise it. Why not exercise and grow that confidence even more?

The result of the growth in your confidence is that it will allow you to try new things.

Is it time to change career paths?

If you have read my first book then you would know that once upon a time, I quit my job to become a fulltime entrepreneur. I saw glitz and glamour in my mind. What I experienced in reality at the time was being fulltime broke. It was not fun, as you would imagine, but hopefully something I will never experience again.

As I further ran into debt, I began to realize that I should get back onto the job market. I kept trying to look for a job but the only companies that got back to me were financial advising firms, and I did not want to get back into doing that. I wanted to do something new.

Eventually, however, I allowed my financial status to dictate my moves and as a result, I went back into financial advising.

Intrinsically, I knew I had to change career paths. I knew I had a superpower when it came to speaking and as I sought to strengthen that further, the idea then came to me to become a professional speaker. I mean, why not? I have the gift! I asked friends that were in the professional speaking circuit what I ought to do to begin. I even used the old sage Google to shed some light on my new interest. Google and my friends made it very clear: I have to write a book on my subject matter of interest, and so I did.

When my first book was eventually published it became the key that opened doors for me that were previously shut. I am now a life, body, and communication coach (author and speech). The book has financed all those qualifications through sales and ad hoc services and products.

If you are looking for a new career, your book has the potential to be that key for you too. But you have to start now or that door will forever remain closed.

> **QUICK QUESTION:**
> Why are you going to write?

Now you know why you ought to write a book. How about some quick tips to remember on your journey as you write?

CHAPTER 7
AS YOU WRITE, REMEMBER...

As you write remember five things:

1. What value is
2. Write to a friend
3. Throw away perfection
4. It will be taxing
5. It will be worthwhile

What value is...

As per Google's definition, value is "the regard that something is held useful"[6].

I have clients who have written books that are heavily researched. I have clients who have done the complete opposite. I have clients who have published their book in color; I have clients that have not. I have clients who have charged huge amounts for their book; I have clients that have not.

---

6   https://www.google.com/search?q=value&oq=calue&aqs=chrome.
     1.69i57j0l5.4832j0j7&sourceid=chrome&ie=UTF-8

I have clients that have written long books; I have clients that have written short books. Some clients have taken years to write their books; there are clients that have taken months.

Where am I going with this?

At the end of the day, neither of these clients is right or wrong. There is no right way or wrong way of publishing a book. The only important question every book must answer is whether or not it gives the reader value. Can the reader take your information and do something useful with it to advance their lives? That is the only question worth answering.

Whether your book is in color or not, long or short, heavily researched or not, expensive or not, it doesn't matter. Your reader just needs to walk away from your book changed for the better.

As you write, people will criticize your work. Remember however that your job is to give value to the customer reading your book. Do not waste time trying to do things that would not answer to that. If the person who is giving you this criticism is not buying your book then please treat their criticism like water off a duck's back.

If, however, this is a customer and they are giving you feedback then listen to them. They have spent their hard-earned finances to enable you to pursue your dreams in exchange for their own value. Their address to you will allow you to grow. Their address will allow you to ensure the next books you author will be better and add more value to your readership.

Write to a friend

As I was writing my first book, I asked for advice from different authors. One piece of advice I received spoke to my heart and shifted my soul.

James Altucher said to me, "Grant, tell people what worked for you and how it may work for them but do not tell them what to do."

This advice inspired me to write as though I am writing to a friend. I advocate that as you write, write as though you are talking to a friend. This is something I always try to implement. Even with the podcast I co-hosted with Marco Jacobs. Why is this important? No one likes to be told what to do. We prefer to figure it out ourselves so we can own the solution and therefore better implement it.

We all already have all the answers to our problems within us. What we do when we read books is to further validate our thoughts and perhaps obtain insights from others.

As you write your book, keep that in mind. The person who reads your book would certainly apply your useful hints much more effectively if they are suggested and not told to do so.

Throw away perfection

Your job as you write is to ensure one day you complete your work of art. Note the word 'complete'.

At one of the writing workshops we ran, I heard an interesting story from one of the delegates that had me and the rest of the delegates laughing. We all however resonated with the moral of the story.

There was a friend of the delegate that wanted to write a book. That person started writing their book and began to look at it and think it was not ready. They thought that more still had to be done, which is reasonable to expect to feel that way too.

He, however, kept working on it year in year out. To this date, it has been six years since he started his journey. Guess what? That book has still not been released.

I also fell into that trap. I started writing a book on sales. I had about 25 000 words as my target. I also wanted perfection, and guess what? That manuscript is still waiting to be turned into a book.

The delegate's friend and I got caught in the trap of pursuing perfection and not completion. There was an inner critic within him and I that would tell us that there is still more to say, there is still more that could be added. Listening to that voice as the years rolled, insured that the idea of publishing gathered dust.

While you are on your journey, I want you to know that there comes a point where you will have to let go of that self-negative talk and publish your book. If anything is missing you can make up for it by writing another book. Matter of fact I doubt any book is fully complete. Generally, once you have offloaded ideas, more come to occupy the space that the others have left behind. Write another book as opposed to elongating the current book you are writing.

Even if you wrote a 'perfect' book you would still have to deal with the fact that a year from now you will look back at your book and think, "What was I thinking?", because as time changes so will you.

Lastly, the longer you wait with your manuscript the longer it will take for it to be released. From a subconscious point of view, you would have entrenched the belief of not completing your manuscript by always wanting to add or subtract words or concepts. Your subconscious will pick this out and will ensure you act accordingly. As you would know, 95% of our decisions are made by our subconscious mind. Don't allow it to keep your manuscript on the shelf indefinitely.

What is the moral of the two stories? Sit down, write your book, and publish it. Waiting for perfection will not serve you in any way. It will only paralyze you from releasing your work of art.

It will be taxing

A client messaged me a few days ago. She is currently writing her book which is due in a few months. By the time this is out, I am certain it would have been published. At the point of writing this, we are currently getting her manuscript prepared for editing. In her message she said, "Grant becoming an author is hard work." I replied, "Wait until you are one, the mountain only gets steeper." We laughed but we both knew at the moment how truthful both statements are.

It is hard work to become an author. There is a lot of work you have to put in to make a book and after the book is complete you still have to follow through with sales and looking to open doors to new opportunities for yourself. There is an underlying commitment you make and have to fulfil.

In becoming an author, you subscribe to a new reality and lifestyle. It will not be easy. If you were looking for easy, then thank you for purchasing this book but perhaps becoming an author should not be something you put your mind, heart, finances or hands to, because it will be taxing.

But on the other hand, however...

It will be worthwhile

At my first book launch, I was ecstatic, above the moon. I had an audience come from all their homes to congratulate me. They came to share in my moment of accomplishment. This is a celebration that will move your soul. When you have completed your book, expect to feel this way.

Apart from the euphoria of your book launch, you will learn something about yourself that I will sum up in two words: you can. Regardless of all the obstacles you have faced that wanted to stop you from reaching and obtaining your goal. You have fought that inner critic every day since you started and now you have a permanent sign of victory. This type of power you cannot buy; you have to earn it and you will.

The discipline you have to have will cause you to realize that you can set your eyes on something and achieve it. So, when the question, "What else can you do?" pops into your mind, you will proudly and promptly respond with, "Anything!"

The growth you would have accomplished as an author is admirable. I, therefore, say, urge and ask that you consider writing that book inside you. Start now, start today and when you complete it you will only be thankful to yourself.

Remember, you have a whole team in my company willing to support you. In the wise words of the famous Michael Jackson let's sing together, "You are not alone." My team and I are with you all the way.

Now you have all the reasons in the world why you should write. When should you start?

Now.

CONCLUSION

For the book inside you to come alive and be of value to a reader, it must have a Golden Thread. The stronger the Golden Thread, the more potential value your reader will experience.

But once you have created a Golden Thread then guess what?

It's time to build a writing schedule.

A writing schedule will ensure you consistently know where you are with your work. This will ensure that when you are behind on the schedule, you know how far back and what to do to ensure you complete your book in time.

Flip the page once more to learn how to set goals and what impeccable techniques and hacks I have to share with you that will further usher your dreams in from aspiring to accomplished author.

LACK OF PROPER GOAL SETTING TECHNIQUES – HOW TO SET WRITING GOALS AND ACHIEVE THEM

"Our goals can only be reached through a vehicle of a plan, in which we must fervently believe, and upon which we must vigorously act. There is no other route to success" – Pablo Picasso

Figure 4 The Five Pillars of Self-Publishing © - Goal Setting

CHAPTER 8
THE VALUE OF
UNCOMPLETED BOOKS

I know I dibbled and dabbled about the negative effects of an uncompleted book but I would like to dive in a tad more.

There are three things that I have experienced in not completing a book:

1. Unchanged lives.
2. Lack of confidence from not finishing something.
3. Resistance to start a new project.

Unchanged lives

Your book is an answer to a problem that you have found a solution to. If it is said that what is specific is general, then it is fair to assume that someone else in the world is facing that same problem. Someone needs your help.

If you do not complete your book that life does not change; this is quite the responsibility to consider before you decide not to publish a book.

Lack of confidence from not finishing something

Confidence is like a muscle. It grows and strengthens upon completion of certain tasks. The size of the task does not matter, just the fact that it is complete will bring in a dose of confidence.

As I speak, as I have previously mentioned, I have a whole sales book that needs to be published. I have decided that after this book is published, the next book in line will be the sales book. I had initially promised that it would be released on the 29th of November 2018. As the date drew nearer, friends would ask me how far I am with the process. Needless to say, I let them know of my progress and then kept silent with embarrassment.

But like a phoenix, I will rise from the ashes of my procrastination.

You can too if you have a manuscript waiting to be transformed into a book.

Resistance to start a new project

Now, remember confidence is a muscle that is meant to help you complete other tasks.

If your confidence takes a knock, that could result in you resisting to take on new challenges. You could remain stuck where you are when there is a whole world waiting to be navigated and conquered. The world is waiting, don't allow it to wait too long.

Your book is also going to become a stepping stone to larger opportunities. If you do not publish your book, who knows what larger opportunities you will miss out on?

Complete your book and keep your confidence growing, which in turn will open up new opportunities for you and give you the confidence to navigate and conquer them.

In order to complete something, however, you have to start hacking at it. The next chapter deals with that in-depth.

QUICK QUESTION:
When is your book going to be published?

CHAPTER 9
ROME WAS NOT BUILT IN A DAY

The value of starting

To complete anything, you have to start. Most people keep ideas in their minds of possible projects that they want to achieve, however, they never start hacking at them. Every year, they have ideas on losing weight, starting a new business or simply making that year the best year of their lives, yet, they never start and the next year the same chorus plays but the stanzas never come.

Imagine your mind pregnant with a plethora of ideas. Now imagine those ideas never being given birth to. That thought always leaves me with a knot in my gut - I hope you felt it too. I challenge you to give those ideas life by diving into the pool of bravery and courage.

From the podcast that I hosted with Marco Jacobs entitled, 'From Potential to Results', we mapped out two things that really stop you from starting anything. These two hindrances are also reiterated in the workshops on book writing that our company runs as well.

The two hindrances are:

1. Fear
2. Doubt

Let's differentiate them.

1. Fear

Fear is when your body responds to something it doesn't understand or actually knows to be dangerous.

Each and every one of us has something that we fear. No one is exempt from fear.

While fear does lurk in our minds and tries to cripple us from propelling forward, we always have the choice to charge after our dreams regardless. Look, the bad news is that the fears we face will never disappear; the good news is that it doesn't matter. If you would like to control your fear, then all you have to do is learn to acknowledge your fear and then choose to overcome it. Do not ignore it like it does not exist. Acknowledge its existence. Once acknowledged, take action by choosing to overcome it. In your mind, the dialogue will sound like this, "I am fearful of ... but it will disappear as I ..."

That sentence will essentially teach you how to manage your fears.

The fear most aspiring authors have is the fact that they do not know something. It is the lack of information that is keeping them fearful. To dig even deeper, the fear you feel is based on the premise of not knowing whether or not your book will be accepted or rejected by people once published.

The sentence I shared with you would then sound like this: "I am fearful of my book being rejected or heavily criticized but it will disappear as I ensure there is a market for the book and under-stand that this is part of the journey of publishing."

Now here is a disclaimer: while you will now be more enlightened to move forward, fear will still lurk in the background of your mind. It will be pleading for your attention but you will starve it consistently with that sentence. This will cause you to just start writing and then eventually publish your book.

What is also important is to remember that your fear is neither negative nor positive. It just is. It's your actions after you feel the fear that takes on the label of negative or positive. If you crumble and fold to fear then you have negatively reacted to it. If you, however, choose to conquer the fear then you have positively reacted to it. "Fear is kind of like the low fuel indicator in your car", Marco once told me. "You don't stop driving your car when you see it flash, instead you add fuel."

As a result, fear to me has now become a huge teddy bear because I understand its purpose. When it rears its head, I march to it vehemently and wholeheartedly embrace it because on the other side of every fear faced, lays my dream for the taking. On the other side of your fear, your dream lays in wait to be taken too. Go and take it.

Fear, however, refuses to come alone. It has an identical twin called doubt.

2. Doubt

Doubt, just like fear, is merely a signal. It is neither negative nor positive.

Most motivational material urges one to tell doubt to shut up, but I think that that is the wrong way of going about it. Instead, as we did with fear, acknowledge the doubt. Acknowledge it by answering any question it asks.

While fear is really about what people perceive of you, doubt deals with what you perceive about yourself. Fear will ask, "Who will read your book?" Doubt will ask, "What qualifies you to become an author?"

One way to circumvent doubt is to use the following sentence: "I may not be qualified now, but I will be when I am done".

You, my fellow author, are in the business of becoming until you become. You may not start out capable and that's fine, but you should know that you will end capable. It's kind of like the bigger-sized clothes our parents buy for us when we are very young with the promise that we will eventually grow into them. You will grow into the role you are becoming, the role of an accomplished author.

> **QUICK QUESTION:**
> How will you respond when fear and doubt come knocking on your door?

While starting is great, it needs a further component. That component is consistency.

CHAPTER 10
CONSISTENCY

For some, starting is easy but remaining consistent becomes very difficult; as a friend of mine would always say, "Everyone has starting power, but few people have staying power."

> **QUICK QUESTION:**
> Do you have 'staying' power?

From my personal experience consistency demands two things:

1. Simplicity
2. Growth

These two elements will either ensure you obtain your goal in publishing your book or they will ensure you never do. The difference between the two results is your decision.

1. Simplicity

Start small when you begin your book. Start with writing something as small as 300 words a day or only write for 10 minutes daily.

You may laugh and scoff at the idea but the truth is that as beautiful as Rome is, it was not built in a day and neither will your book. Rome was built brick by brick and the bricks to your book are your words. Starting small will help you with the confidence it takes to start and will not overwhelm you with your vision of publishing from the onset.

A friend of mine, Ntsundeni Ndou, fellow author and professional speaker, began his book by opening a file on his desktop and naming it "Project: 1 Page a Day". He is an author now.

Start small if you wish to see huge results.

QUICK QUESTION:
How will you start small?

2. Growth

When you begin to get the handle of being consistent, you will feel the urge to challenge yourself to do more.

As these expectations rise, I challenge you to demand more from yourself. You would at this point have grown the confidence, so how about we flex those muscles and ensure they don't suffer from atrophy?

I used to only write for 10 minutes a day when I first started out. On the day I typed this section, I have been writing for 3 hours non-stop. I am not more blessed than you are, and what I did you can achieve too by simply repeating the same. Start small then demand more.

Another important point to note is the definition of consistency. Consistency is merely when you are frequent at doing something. That means that you could write daily or you could write three times a week. It's completely your choice. Whatever you pick, however, remember to keep to it.

Also, carve out the time to find moments to rest. My partner Anna and my life coach Sonia always remind me of this. I love to work and separating me from my work can sometimes bring an avalanche of anxiety. This is because I believe one's work is a gift from God and God wants us to fully utilize what He has given us. Take note that a job and work are different. A job is there to sustain you while work is there to fulfil you. A job is merely for necessities, while work is about your purpose.

Anyhow, what I have learned with time is that having intentional breaks in your writing will ensure that your mind rests. This rest will cause new and creative ideas to flow and rise to the surface. In the book *Mastery* by Robert Greene, he proves the point that everyone that has attained mastery has had those breaks, and it is within these breaks that great ideas are formed. These ideas may have the capability to breathe life into your work or give it a good revamp. So do find time to rest.

The resting process can also be likened to taking your car in for a service. A service ensures that your car is still fit to run for longer distances. Apply the same principle to yourself. Writing and publishing a book is a process; you are in it for the long haul. Find the time to rest so you can complete your journey without getting burnt out.

At this point, you have learned the value of starting and becoming consistent. What completes this thought is finally learning how to finish.

The art of finishing

It takes just as much control and self-discipline to stop something as it does to start and keep consistent with it.

How will you know when that time comes for you? You will know this by ensuring that you have set your target number of words upfront as opposed to just writing and figuring things out along the way. Is the number of words set in stone? No. It only serves as a good indicator upfront and allows you to gauge your performance.

QUICK QUESTION:
How many words will your book
consistent of?

Once you have an answer to the above question then all that is left is to begin, then to keep consistent, and finally to finish.

As you begin your journey, how about I share with you some hacks to make you churn those words faster?

CHAPTER 11
WRITING FASTER

The methods that I am going to be sharing with you are all going to work. I know that because I have used them time and time again and our company has enabled people to use the same tools time and time again.

I would advise you to take it easy by not diving into the pool and using all the tools at once. Instead, ease into it. Once you feel a sense of mastery then go ahead to the next one and the one thereafter too.

Let's start with how you are going to write. You could either:

1. Sprint
2. Transcribe

Take note that I did not have conventional writing because this chapter is about writing faster. Conventional writing will not aid you in this regard. If anything, it will cause you to take much longer than necessary.

Enough talk let's get into the first method of writing fast, sprinting.

1. Sprinting

Learning this method of writing has allowed me to churn more words than I would have typed conventionally.

But before I show you how to sprint and what it is, let me share with you why you ought to.

Why sprint?

You were blessed with a brilliant mind that can-do extraordinary things and can create just about anything.

What your brilliant brain has difficulty doing is writing and editing at the same time. This is because our brain is divided into two: the left and the right hemisphere.

The left hemisphere

The left hemisphere of the brain is in charge of the right side of the body. It also performs tasks that have to do with logic, such as science or mathematics. In the case of your book and your writing, the left hemisphere of your brain does the editing and critical thinking of both your words and your ideas.

An interesting thought is how the left hemisphere of the brain controls the right side of the body, which makes sense as to why your right hand is closest to the back-space button. Could this be a mere coincidence? I highly doubt it.

The right hemisphere

The right hemisphere of your brain controls the left side of your body and performs tasks that have to do with creativity and arts. In the case of writing your book, it is responsible for the ideas that you are putting onto the page in front of you.

Grant, so what?

Great question! As you write you are engaging the right side of your brain. You are getting all the ideas you have onto a page. When you edit and critically think through your work you are engaging the left side of your brain.

Trying to do both at one go will only leave you with fewer words on your screen. A second reason not to engage both is the fact that there are ideas you will forget along the way causing you to stare at a blank screen at times. This is where writers' block can potentially emanate from.

So, as you sprint, remember that now is not the time for editing. Now is the time for sprinting, anything else will simply slow you down.

What is sprinting?

Sprinting is when you begin to write your thoughts down onto a page without stopping to press the backspace button or to correct your grammar. You do this for a specified amount of time. You could use your phone as a timer or anything else at your disposal.

Your screen will have a bunch of red, blue, and green underlining. Not to worry, you will come back to that at a future date. The point right now is to transport the ideas from your mind onto the page in front of you.

Remember your focus is to ensure you build momentum by finishing your first manuscript in the shortest amount of time. That momentum will catapult you to getting your book published faster.

Here are some tips I believe would help you as you sprint:

1. Remove all distractions.
2. Celebrate only after you have achieved a milestone.
3. Measure everything.

Remove all distractions

While you are sprinting, you do not want anything to disturb you. They are two reasons for this.

You will be measuring how many words you have churned and you want to keep your ideas flowing.

During your sprinting time tell your friends, family, and colleagues not to disturb you for the amount of time that you would be sprinting for. If they complain, bribe them with a mention in the acknowledgments for your book as a token for them supporting you.

Celebrating milestones

By now you should have a ballpark figure of how long you would want your book to be. Cut that up into quarters and every time you reach a quarter, celebrate. My life coach, Sonia, keeps reminding me how celebrating will get your body and mind to enjoy this process.

It will associate writing as a good thing and keep you motivated.

I have tried it. Sonia is right, it will lead you to great results. As I wrote this section, I was en route to 10 000 words. Once I get there, I am going to celebrate. It may be as simple as buying a ticket to a self-development event or taking Anna out for dinner. Heck, maybe even both! Then again, I should perhaps confirm with my bank account first.

As I check my bank account, figure out how you would like to celebrate and which milestones will be worth it for you.

QUICK QUESTION:
How will you celebrate milestones?

Measure everything

As said in the section above you should have your number of words by now, all written out. What you would want to do with these measurements is to figure out how many hours it would take for you to get to the number of words you were looking to reach. Once you know that, then you know how many times you would need to sit down and for how long too.

At one of the workshops, we managed to show delegates that if you sit down and sprint for 30 minutes, 36 times, you will have your first manuscript in front of you. Think about it, to create the magic of your first manuscript is a matter of sitting down 36 times for 30 minutes consistently. This is if the number of words in your book is 30 000. If your book is longer or shorter you need only to manipulate the numbers.

Each time the team and I present this in the workshops that we run, the delegates look amazed and enthused. The reality of them publishing a book seizes to be farfetched. They see their dream of becoming an accomplished author edge closer toward them.

When should you begin sprinting?

Only sprint once you have completed your Golden Thread. In an exercise that we run at our workshops; we do two sprinting exercises.

The first is just to get them acquainted with how to sprint and then they are given a random subject to sprint on.

The second time we take the same random topic they wrote about in the first exercise and we structure it better. The result is that 80% of the class always has more words on their screens. Now, this can come down to the fact that they have done the exercise before and therefore they are now a well-oiled machine.

More times than not, however, you will write more because you have structure and therefore your thoughts are now aligned to something specific. Your brain will then pinpoint and reveal all the things it knows around that subject matter. Specific will always trump general.

What happens to the other 20% that write more words in the first exercise as opposed to the second? I have narrowed it down to two things:

1. The topic chosen is not one that they are well acquainted with therefore when the second exercise commences because it has more structure to something they do not know, the words churned are less. This, however, will not be the case for you because you will write about what interests you.

2. The second reason is because of the enormous pressure they put on themselves. They look at the timer and think, "Oh, I have to type, I have to type, I have to type!" My advice to you here is simple. Write in a relaxed state, take it easy. Tap the keys instead of punching them and you will churn out more words. The more relaxed you are, the faster the words will churn. I am not too sure why, but I am very confident of this having seen it in my own sprinting.

What to sprint on?

Your Golden Thread should be laid out in front of you while you sprint; this is a non-negotiable.

Just as you are about to sprint, I want you to look at your Golden Thread. I want you to concentrate on just what you will be sprinting on. Once you have a good idea, it's time to sprint.

As you type, focus on the present moment. Don't think of the next chapter or the paragraph prior to the one you are unleashing. Just keep your mind focused on what you are going to be typing. This will get you to churn more words because your thoughts are focused.

I divide my screen into two. I write on the right half of the screen. My Golden Thread which I have expressed as a mind map, I keep on the left side of the screen. I look at one idea and I sprint like my life depends on it. As soon as I feel my mind beginning to say, "I think we have exhausted everything", I take a look at the next section of the mind map and subsequently hop onto the next paragraph. This allows the flow of typing and ideas to continue unperturbed.

There is however a faster way to reach your word count in the same amount of time that you would take to sprint.

2. Transcribing

When I started writing my first book, I would hear of how some authors would have up to 80 books under their belts. Yes, you heard right, 80!

Like you, I would wonder where they got the time to write that many.

Upon further research I then discovered that it was not a matter of time, it was a matter of speed. Most of these authors were not writing their first manuscript. They were speaking it into existence. They were transcribing it.

Knowing this, upon visiting a client of mine I decided to try it out. I asked her to run three exercises:

1. Write conventionally.
2. Sprint.
3. Transcribe.

The time limit for each of those exercises was 3 minutes.

When she wrote conventionally, she came to about 61 words. When she sprinted, she came up with 152 words. When she transcribed, she came up with 455 words.

If you had to write a barrage of books, which method would you use?

Since that moment I have never looked back. For the first manuscript, I always pick transcription. Always.

You would follow the exact procedure you would when sprinting. You would have your

Golden Thread in front of you at all times and all you would do is talk through it. The app I use is an app called *'Live Transcribe'*. I have noticed however that this app is mainly for Android users. For Apple consumers, you may have to find another app. Email me at info@thegoldengooseinstitute.com if and when you do. It will help the dozens of Apple clients that we would receive.

Transcribing however is really only worth its salt when you want to complete the first manuscript. When editing, you would return to the basics. Going through each sentence and thought to ensure you dig out the diamonds in your thoughts and ideas.

Whether you decide to transcribe or not is up to you. In our workshops, we have even had people that would prefer to write on paper as opposed to use any form of technology. Do what suits you best, my job is to show the possibilities and to shed light on the timeline you have.

QUICK QUESTION:
Which method of writing will you use?

You could write your book conventionally and by that, I mean word for word, however, it will take you a while to complete.

Alternatively, you could sprint. Sprinting will ensure you complete your book faster. If you really want to up the ante further, then I would recommend you transcribe.

Remember that the latter two are just for you to get past your first manuscript. After the first manuscript is complete, then it is time to edit and add any other additional material as well.

Completing your first manuscript should take you no less than a month. Your first manuscript should take the least time when it comes to the process of developing your book.

What really takes up a lot of your time is editing. This is the part that the left hemisphere of your brain has been waiting for.

CHAPTER 12
EDITING

This for me is the most tiring bit of the book. The key to success here is repetition and patience. This is also where you learn your work verbatim. However, grueling this process is, I can tell you this from experience; it is at this point that your book begins to take form. What started as a dark piece of coal steadily becomes a diamond before your very eyes.

Let me tell you why.

The importance of editing

The first time you write down anything, you will write in such a manner that only you will understand.

What an editor does is that they take your ideas and begin to make them ready for someone else to read and understand too. What initially only made sense to you now makes sense to someone else.

Content editing vs proofreading

Content editing is really making sure your ideas make sense to other readers. It is also about the development of your ideas throughout your book. On the other hand, proofreading is about syntax and grammar. Proofreading focuses on how your ideas are expressed through words.

Both are paramount. These two types of edits can be broken up into two types of editors: a developmental editor and a proof-reader. As you begin to look for editors ensure you have someone that can do both of those. It will save you money in regards to the cost of your book.

Who should edit your work?

A professional; not a friend nor someone who you can have to do pro bono work.

Your book will fall or rise depending on the editing. Sidestepping this will be at your demise.

This part of the book is also where the bulk of your money is usually spent. The second is printing. Take a deep breath and pay the editor what is due to them. It will come back to you twofold.

To ensure that you also have an editor that is worth their weight in gold, ask for work they have done before. If you can, have physical evidence from the editor as to what a manuscript looked like before they edited versus after they did. You need not read a full manuscript, perhaps just a chapter or two. The difference between the two manuscripts should be worth every penny you spend their way. If you feel the difference does not warrant the amount, they are charging you, look for another editor until you get one you feel is worth it.

When to begin editing

A friend of mine who is a professional editor mentioned how one of his pet peeves is when someone hands him their first manuscript and apart from editing, he has to rewrite the whole thing. Please do not be the person my friend was talking about.

Here is what I would advise; once you are done with your first manuscript, I want you to go through it and edit it yourself at least three times.

The first time

I want you to do so looking at grammar and spelling. Once you have cleaned up the document, then we'd move into step two.

The second time

Step two is really about looking for more ideas to add, which would come from your research of other material (more on that later). This is also where you make your stories better by adding details and putting more life into your work. This will take you some time and I encourage you to welcome it because it will cause your book to rise in the quality of its ideas.

The third time

The third and final step is when you go through your work and ask yourself two questions.

1. Why would someone care about this? What value does this sentence or paragraph add to the reader? Remember, value here is measured by the usefulness of the material. If it is useful, keep it. If it is not, trash it. To make this work, leave your ego out of the room for this and put your reader first.

2. How does one-chapter link into the next? The point of this question is to ensure the reader does not stop reading your book and continues from chapter to chapter. At the end of all your chapters, find creative ways to get them to continue reading into the next chapter.

Ensure you do each solely. If done at the same time it can cause your work to end up being muddled from trying on too many lenses at one go. It will also take longer to finish because of the consistent starting and stopping. The key to making this work is in the fact that each time you come to your work you will have a different lens to look at it through.

If you have any trouble with this, send us an email. We have in-house editors that would be willing to do your work.

QUICK QUESTION:
Who is your editor going to be?

Let's now transition and put in place a timeline for your book.

CHAPTER 13
TIMELINES

Firstly, you would have to complete your Golden Thread, which should take at most three weeks to a month.

In week one you would understand what the goal of your book would be.

In week two you would then figure out what problem your book solves.

In weeks three and four, you would work out at least ten causes of the problem you wish to solve and the three to five solutions to every cause. During this phase it is important to also address what the gaps in your knowledge are so you can further research them.

You are now officially 30 days in with our Golden Thread. Next is churning out the first manuscript.

Churning your manuscript is really the magic trick that ensures your book actualises. So, before you head onto the next section, I want you to stretch, grab a beverage of your liking and ensure the room is silent as I am about to go into a surmountable amount of detail.

Churning your first manuscript

An average Joe or Jane would type 2 000 words per hour. Let's work according to Joe and Jane.

If your book is 30 000 words long, and you only have 30 minutes to write per day then it should take you 30 days to finish your first manuscript. Let's add another two weeks for contingencies. So that means we have our initial manuscript in 44 days.[7]

At this point, you have done your Golden Thread and you have completed your first manuscript in two months and two weeks. Well done!

You will also have done some research. Based on the assumption that it takes 3 books to become a knowledgeable expert in a given field; if every book is 30 000 words, it would take you 30 hours to complete all three. If you read 30 minutes a day, it will take you 60 days to finish all 3 books. The time for this research would ideally be immediately after you have completed your Golden Thread and

---

7   Just as a matter of interest you could half that time if you transcribe. For the sake of evening the playing field however, we are going with worst case scenario.

therefore you would have 16 days of reading left after your first manuscript. Also, take note that at the end of the day you do not need to read an entire book. You need only read what is most applicable to your book.

These days of reading will seep into your editing.

You will edit the book 3 times. This should take you a good month, being 30 days before you send it off to a professional editor. Within that time, however, you would have read the books you need to and met with the relevant experts if there was a need to as well.

By the time you have your first edited manuscript, you would be on day 98.

You would need to get reviews and a foreword on your book and I would give that a month as well. You could speed this process up by letting the reviewers know that they should just read a few chapters to get the essential message. If your Golden Thread has been done well, then this will not be a problem. At this point, you should be at 128 days. You are four months in. You now have an edited manuscript; you have your reviews and foreword.

During the 30 days between your edited manuscript and when you receive your reviews and foreword, you will have time to work on a cover, set a book launch date, and know how long the printers will take to print your book.

The only thing that could perturb you would be a lack of finances to do everything this smoothly. If your finances are in order then this is your timeline.

You will begin marketing your book as soon as your manuscript has been professionally edited. The marketing will start from that final manuscript all the way until your book launch and thereafter. I will show you how to do this in the last section of this book.

Your worst-case scenario is that you spend 5 months on the first couple of steps which would result in leaving you with a whole 7 months to work with. If your book is longer, I would suggest you write for longer and close off all distractions. Ask for that support during this time. If you cannot type that fast, then type for much longer. Whatever the case, drop the excuses and take the time to make this work! The future version of you will be thankful that you positioned them differently and allowed them more options in life.

This is how you write a book in a year. It is possible. Below is a graphical presentation of your journey to actualising your idea into a book within a year.

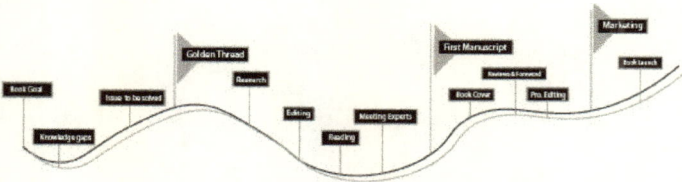

Figure 5 Steps to writing and publishing a book ©

QUICK QUESTION:
What is the timeline that you will be working with?

Want additional hacks that could make your writing process even faster? Flip to the next chapter.

CHAPTER 14
HOW TO WRITE EVEN FASTER

Before I get into the tips of how to write faster, I would like to present you with a way to set goals that aid you through this process.

For eons, we have been told to set S.M.A.R.T. goals. If you are hearing of this for the first time, S.M.A.R.T is an acronym that stands for Smart, Measurable, Attainable, Realistic, and Time-based. While I agree with that acronym, what I have realized with time is how static that way of setting goals is. It also really deals with goals in an isolated manner, and we all know goals are never achieved in isolation. It takes more than just your efforts to achieve a goal. You need people to help you. There are more reasons why you ought to change your goal methodology and you can find out more in an article by MIT Sloan Management Review entitled "With Goals, FAST beats SMART"[8].

Here are my reasons, but first some descriptions.

---

8   https://sloanreview.mit.edu/article/with-goals-fast-beats-smart/

F.A.S.T. goals

F.A.S.T. is an acronym for Frequently discussed, Ambitious, Specific, and Transparent.

1. *Frequently discussed*

Goals need to be frequently discussed. This would mean that you need either to get an accountability partner or start a mastermind.

An accountability partner is someone that would keep you accountable. They need not be trying to accomplish the same thing that you are although from my experience I have seen how it would help more having someone who wants to achieve what you are looking to achieve too. You are able to share experiences.

With a mastermind the same rules apply, the only difference is that there is a group of people. The benefits of having an accountability partner amplify within a mastermind.

Both these options will allow you to keep an account of what you need to accomplish. If you have picked an accountability partner or mastermind on the same journey as you, then based on the shared experiences you could also find new ways to accomplish your goal.

I have two accountability partners as we speak. I speak to both every Monday to discuss their progress with their goals and my progress as well. This consistent follow up keeps me consistently alert as to whether or not I am progressing. More importantly, it teaches me to build an awareness of what is working for me and what is not. That awareness will catapult you through this journey faster.

The other added benefit is that sharing your goals will also mean you get the opportunity to have other people give you ideas that could assist you to reach your goal faster through their resources. This is irrespective of whether they are walking on the same journey as you or not. Living inside your head with your goals will slow you down.

Find a trusted circle to share your goals with.

2. *Ambitious*

Whatever you plan to achieve, it must challenge your core. Your goal must stretch you beyond what you would have the ability to accomplish. If it does not challenge you, you will not grow.

In terms of your book, set ridiculous deadlines. Then as you think and ponder on how to achieve them, your mind will begin to open avenues to you that you otherwise would have never considered. The question is, will you listen?

3. Specific

Your goals need to be measured by metrics. Metrics are what make goals specific. I could say I want to be an author one day. Great wish, terrible goal. "By 31st December 2020, I will be an author of a book consisting of 30 000 words." That is a great goal and it has specific metrics that you can measure. The other importance of these metrics is that if you can't measure your goals using them then how will you know whether you are progressing or not?

Every moment when I write, I record what I am writing about: I record what time I am writing. I record how long I will write for. I record how many words I started with. I record how many I have ended with. I then calculate the difference.

This allows me to have a base for my writing and as a result, when I want to write a book, I have metrics to help me through the process.

That's not the only benefit. Having metrics also allows you to manipulate things. What do I mean by that? You can start looking at more efficient and effective ways of writing that will get you to your goal faster. This is where your ambition will propel you leaps and bounds by aiding you with new ideas, hacks, or techniques.

Challenge yourself by recording and using metrics.

4. *Transparent*

Keep your goals somewhere you can see them clearly. It would serve as a constant reminder to you. These reminders will also spark creative ways of completing your goals by adding consistent pressure on you.

As is, I have my goals on my wall. I have my values, personal mission, and vision there too. I also have a vision board. All this transparency ensures that I remember what is important and why I ought to complete the tasks I set.

In your case with your book, why not print out the title of your book and place it somewhere public? That reminder will get you active. Try it, feel it, and then feel free to get back to me about your results.

Now you have a methodology to work within concerning your book.

Next, I discuss hacks in detail.

Tips, tricks, and hacks to make writing faster

You should have mapped out your Golden Thread by now. This means that you would have also outlined the chapters within your book as well. If you haven't, then this section may not be as valuable. Perhaps do so before reading any further?

I will now give you the five tips that have helped me, but if you want more, I would advise you to read Daniel Hall's book *Read Fast Writing*[9]. He has 25 tips that could get you to write faster.

Here are mine:

1. *Begin with a quote*

Start your chapter with a quote. This quote must be specific to the chapter that you will be writing on.

2. *Have a picture*

In my first book, I had a picture for every chapter. A quote may work well if you are someone like me that loves words. If you are more of a visionary person then I would advise you to pick a picture for every chapter. It will spur on further creativity.

---

[9] https://www.amazon.com/Real-Fast-Writing-Easy-Implement/dp/0943941008

In addition to the above, what I also like about having a quote or a picture would be the fact that your page does not look empty when you are about to begin writing. This allows your mind to know you are not starting from scratch because we all know the amount of effort it takes to begin something. Your page is simply pleading with you to continue as opposed to starting.

3. Set the trim size

I do this one all the time. Trim your word document page to the size you imagine your book will be.

What this tip will do is allow you to know how many pages you have written. It excites me to see this because I begin to feel as though my book is taking form. When I wrote this section, I started on page 48. Now I am on page 52. Each new page I complete excites me to want to write more. It will do the same for you too.

Try it.

4. Accountability partner & mastermind

I covered the importance of having an accountability partner earlier on and the benefit it will have on your writing. Here I want to delve into having a mastermind.

A mastermind is a group of people who are seeking the same thing as you. In your case, you are seeking to write a book. I would urge you to look for a group of people who want exactly the same thing as you. Let them know what your goal is, and get them to keep you accountable.

What an accountability partner will do for you, a mastermind will amplify. Every book on how to write a book I have come across elaborates on the importance of this. In *Think and Grow Rich* by Napoleon Hill, this concept is highlighted as well. Look, if it's good for Napoleon Hill and the multitude of other experts on becoming an author then it is good enough for me. At our workshops, we offer the delegates the opportunity to form a mastermind group with each other.

5. Affirmations

We are the words we repeat to ourselves. If ever you do not complete a task or fall short of your expectations, check the words that you are using. You will find in more ways than one, they are negative and thus limiting you to reach your full potential.

It is the same with writing your book. There will be negative voices that will surface in your mind. Fear not, this is very natural. What you can do to combat this is to simply have an affirmation for yourself, in response to the messages relayed by the negative voices.

I have several. The one I use for my writing is, "I find it easy to write profusely." I read this daily.

For you to build your affirmation all you need to do is make whatever you are affirming a present tense. It has to be something you have already accomplished.

The second element is your affirmation must be written in the first person. It must start with "I" because this is dealing with you and only you.

The last element is that your affirmation should be made in the positive. "I find it easy to write profusely" is far more effective and propelling than "I find it hard not to write profusely". Your subconscious will allow you to write faster using the first affirmation but the latter will make it harder for you to do so. To be safe with your subconscious say what you mean in the shortest and simplest way.

A new thing we have introduced is having the affirmation "I AM AN AUTHOR" written on a cue card. Delegates are then asked to laminate that card and look at it at least three times a day. From coaching my clients, I can tell you this much: the difficulty that lies in authorship is not in the writing, it is in believing you are indeed an author even before your book is printed. Remember, every goal is lived out twice; once in your mind and the second in reality. The stronger it is in your mind initially, the easier it is to produce in reality.

6. A vision board

I have my vision board placed on the right side of my bed. Every morning I wake up, I have a look at it. It reminds me of where I want to go. It reminds me of who I am becoming. All the pictures there signify something and bring a warm feeling to my heart. The point, however, of this vision board is just to ensure that you are consistently looking at your dreams and fostering a relationship with them. The stronger the positive relationship between you and what you want, the easier it will flow your way.

Disclaimer

All the above tips and tricks to make your writing quick will do so. Please be patient with them as you put them to work.

These techniques are like a water pump. You push up and down, up and down, and initially, no water runs but after you have pushed up and down for a while, the water will begin to flow slowly.

At this point do not fall into the trap of seizing to pump. Continue to pump and as a result, your water will run out of the faucet faster, and you will not have to pump as hard anymore.

It is the same with the above techniques. Pick a few and use them consistently, the results will follow. The writing will flow and become easier.

QUICK QUESTION:
What methods will you use to write faster?

CONCLUSION

At this point, you have what it takes to set proper goals, what will motivate you to write faster, and what will cause your writing to enter a state of flow.

To make your content rise in the level of quality, you will need to do some research. Let's discuss that next.

To make your content rise in the level of quality, you will need to do some research. Let's discuss that next.

LACK OF IN-DEPTH RESEARCH – HOW TO DO THE RESEARCH

"Without data, you're just another person with an opinion." – W. Edwards Deming

Figure 6 The Five Pillars of Self-Publishing © - Research

To become a brilliant writer, you need to be well-read.

There is no circumventing this. When I am approached by a prospect who is interested in writing and publishing a book, I always try to find out how much they read.

Wanting to write a book but not being well-read is like trying to give water out of a dry well. You can only give what you have.

You might ask, "I get you Grant, but what if I am doing an autobiography? Surely all the research that I need is looking at me in the mirror?" You are right, it is, although what could raise the level of content quality in your book can be dependent on other autobiographies that you would have read. I can almost guarantee that your expression through your written words will better articulate the ideas you wish to share. This will translate to your book rising in both quality and value to the reader.

If you are not an avid reader, begin that journey now. This action will not only prove valuable to the book that you are writing now but it will also determine how seamlessly your second, third, and fourth book flow through you.

I am at a point in my life where I can read two to three books a week. The fact that this is a habit for me allows me to draw on knowledge very quickly when I begin typing. It has made my writing easier and I'm certain it will do exactly the same for you.

Won't research drown my voice?

You may think that doing research may drown your voice within your book. That is an understandable conclusion but not a truthful one at its core. If you have a Golden Thread, then your voice is already loud and clear. The research will simply fine-tune it.

Apart from the books that you would need to read, I would also advise that you do some behavioral assessments on how you naturally communicate.

CHAPTER 15
HOW DO YOU COMMUNICATE?

In Tim LaHaye's book, **Why You Act the Way You Do**[10], he highlights four personality types.

Every one of us has all these personalities within us. We, however, lead with one dominantly. How you communicate is based on your primary and secondary personalities. These personalities are as follows:

1. Sanguine,
2. Choleric,
3. Melancholy
4. or Phlegmatic.

Each of these personalities communicates differently. How they communicate often seeps into their writing.

Sanguines are natural storytellers and seek to entertain. When they sit down to write, this will be

_____

10   https://www.amazon.com/Why-You-Act-Way-Do/dp/0842382127

apparent in their way of writing. You will feel their easy-going nature and will emotionally get roped into their stories, time and time again. In our DISC assessments, these are known as "High I's".

Cholerics are straight to the point. They communicate from an authoritative point of view and therefore their books will tell you what to do as opposed to suggest it. Expect shorter reads from them but in that same breath expect a heavy amount of impact. This is my predominant personality. In our DISC assessments, these are known as "High D's". I am a High D.

The Melancholy is detail orientated. They want to know why and understand things to their bare essentials. Their work would be highly detailed with a plethora of references to their ideas and thoughts. Expect a high amount of researched work in their writings. In our DISC assessments, these are known as "High C's".

Phlegmatics are soft-spoken and very relationship orientated. They will rarely express themselves authoritatively and will orientate their wording in a soft-spoken manner to you. Their writing is welcoming and friendly. In our DISC assessments, these are known as "High S's".

In our company, we ensure every aspiring author does an assessment to figure out which they are.

This then allows them to understand who would naturally resonate with their writing and who may struggle with it.

So if you are Sanguine (High I), the Phlegmatic (High S) may love your writing but the Choleric (High D) may want you to cut straight to the point and the Melancholy (High C) may want you to have facts to back your stories up.

You see, understanding this from the onset allows you to manage how you will incorporate other personalities in your writing. Not to appease them but to simply consider them.

So, when you have the time, find out about your personality type so you begin to understand how you communicate and how that would affect readers of different personality types.

The result of this exercise is twofold beneficial. It would allow you to connect further with those that have the same personality type as you and it could allow you to connect with a larger audience too.

Let's now get into how to research your book by starting with what you should research.

CHAPTER 16
SO, WHAT TO RESEARCH?

The first thing you would want to research is whether there is a market for what you would want to write. There are two ways you can go about this:

1. Surveys, forums, or online groups.
2. Just publish!

Here's a little more about both.

1. Surveys, forums, or online groups

You could conduct surveys using Survey Monkey as a platform to collate your results, amongst many other platforms. Your survey should include questions that seek to discover whether there is a need for your book or not. Personally, I find this exercise to be very subjective, however, if you are hell-bent on ensuring you do some research then this is the first option.

The second option would be to look at forums such as Quora for groups of people that are facing the problem you wish to solve. On Quora, one person or a group of people will ask a question and whoever can view that question may go ahead and answer it. If you see questions that would relate to your Golden Thread then this website will certainly be worthwhile for you to explore. To maximize on its value, reflect on the questions people are asking and then have a look at the responses shared. I am certain you will find one or two more things you could add to your book.

Then there is Amazon. Have a look at Amazon and see how many other authors in your genre there are. The more books there are in your category or genre the more money you are likely to make. It may be argued that you will be in stiff competition with other authors within that category but the truth is that you won't. Avid readers buy a lot of books on one subject to understand it holistically. To take advantage of such an opportunity you would just have to ensure your book stands out. A great cover, with reviews, can do this for you.

Facebook groups are a great source too. There are a plethora of Facebook groups that would benefit from your thoughts but also where you could benefit from theirs as well. Just be sure not to join only to sell. I would advise that you rather add value first on a consistent basis and then look at selling when the inquiries keep seeping in. The more inquiries seep in, the more you are assured that there is a market for your book.

Lastly, you can go ahead and speak to experts in your relevant field as well. They would not only be able to guide you by letting you know whether there is a market or not, but they would also be able to show you how to capitalize on it as well.

Disclaimer

While the above tactics are useful, at the end of the day it can be very time-consuming. I would also want you to know that just because there is a market does not necessarily mean that they will buy from you. People may raise their hands and mention how your book will do or can do well, but when it's time to buy, they are nowhere to be seen. So, as you research, keep in mind that while the possibility of sales is evident, whether it will translate to sales is another ball game on its own and that ball game is governed by different rules and activities. Namely, these activities are your marketing efforts which we will touch on in the last section of this book.

2. Just publish!

This is the more expensive route, but the feedback here is real-time. You will know whether people do like your book or not. As they make their opinions known to you, change accordingly, and start fitting yourself to the market. Now, you could do this for the current book you have published by publishing a second edition of the same book or you could use that feedback for your next book.

I know that the method of just publishing sounds gung-ho but I can assure you, waiting on the side-lines for the perfect time will keep you there until the final whistle. Get in the game, make the mistakes, get back up, and do things differently.

I can humbly disclose that there is a lot more research I could have done with my first book, but the feedback I received from actual buyers was worth more to me. It allowed me to change things within that book. This is from the cover to the interior layout. Remember that self-publishing allows you to adapt and I think that is more important to do in the larger scheme of your book life.

Do keep in mind that if this approach makes the knots in your stomach even more nervous, send us an email at info@thegoldengooseinstitute.com. We would be more than happy to mentor, coach, or consult you through this process.

A mix of both perhaps?

If you can, I would advise you to do a mix of both. Do the relevant research but cap the amount of time that you would be spending on it. Otherwise, you may just keep researching perpetually. When you do finally publish, remember that you are starting a journey. That means with the real-time feedback you receive; you need to be agile by going back to the drawing board and returning with a better market fit of a book for the audience you wish to serve.

Apart from researching the market place, another important point of research would be to research for the gaps in your book. These gaps are the pieces of knowledge that you are not acquainted or familiar with.

So, where are the gaps?

We all have scotomas. These are things we are not aware of. When you have stretched your Golden Thread, these scotomas will become apparent to you. It would then be your job to fill that gap with the relevant information. As I mentioned in prior sections of this book, this is when you begin to develop into becoming an expert.

One of the clients I helped publish filled in her gaps very well. Her book was very well researched. There was a chapter however that struck at the strings of my heart and mind. I was so moved that I personally asked her to ensure she makes a keynote out of that chapter. That is the impact of research! The value you add to your reader truly magnifies.

Also remember that the purpose of the research is to let the reader know that you are not the only one with your thoughts, that there are other people on the same wavelength as well. Whether you know it or not, the reader always appreciates this.

Other authors?

Another great source for research to fill your gaps and enlighten your scotomas would be fellow authors within your field. It is important to know what their thoughts are. Knowing their thoughts will give you a gauge as to how on-track you are. By knowing and understanding their thoughts you get the opportunity to know what is missing from their work. That then gives you an opportunity. You will also see bits and pieces of their work that show up in yours.

> **QUICK QUESTION:**
> Where are the gaps of knowledge in
> your Golden Thread?

The audience you wish to serve, are they a niche group or a general audience? Let's discuss that next.

CHAPTER 17
NICHE OR GENERAL AUDIENCE?

A niche is a small market of a well-defined audience e.g. Women wearing black hats every Monday between 09h00 and 10h00. A general audience would be people who wear hats.

Most industry experts will ask you to pick a niche. I agree, but I advise you do not do this from the onset. Start general by selling your book to everyone and anyone. As people begin to buy your book, you are to listen to what they have to say about your book. While you are listening to the market place, I would like you to take note of the people that are consistently buying your book. If you can, try and engage them further; this would not only help you in selling more copies but it will allow you to start building an avatar for your book.

I know that I have stated this idea very simplistically but I can assure you that it is not easy. It takes time, dedication, willingness, and paying attention to detail when it comes to your customers. If you are in this for the long haul then this simple action will reap unimaginable rewards. This would be both from a financial and impact perspective.

After the second workshop we hosted, I decided to make a 16-second promotional video for the third and fourth workshops for the year. This video only had women in it. It was not long until I received feedback from men asking why they were not represented in the promotional video. It was then that I shared the stats with them, as a matter of interest.

We have 15 people attend a workshop. Out of the 15 people that attend only 3 of the 15 are men. In all of our workshops, only two men have come without being referred to the event by a woman. The rest are usually referrals from women attending the workshop.

It is, therefore, safe to say that women are more interested in our workshops and services. To get to that point, however, we had to start by inviting everyone and anyone. If we had picked prematurely, having sold out workshops would have not been evident.

When I look at my first book, the same rules apply.

The moral of the story is not to presume by picking your market prematurely. Start general and include everyone and anyone. In time your market will come to you.

> **QUICK QUESTION:**
> Are you serving a niche or a general audience?

What to research has been covered and you now know what approach to have when it comes to the audience you are looking to serve.

Let's delve into how you should do your research.

CHAPTER 18
HOW TO RESEARCH –
THE RULE OF THREE

Rule No 1: Other authors

Find three books for every chapter that you are working on. Books that really zone in on the material your chapter is sharing. I would personally advise taking up a reading course so you can speed read through all these books. Udemy was where I completed my speed-reading course. I encourage you to enrol, it will be one of the best investments you will make.

The reason I would want you to speed read is that what you are looking for is specific and therefore you do not need to read a whole book in-depth, merely the parts that matter most.

Rule No 2: What are the experts saying?

Are there any experts that would also validate your thoughts, ideas, or concepts?

How To Do The Research

While the books you read may have great information, the application of that information may be outdated.

What experts in your subject matter do is that they keep you abreast with the application of your information.

While I was still a financial planner, I remember having read 3 books on cold calling. They were great. The only problem I faced was how people I called had Truecaller ID installed on their mobile devices. So, when I would call from my office line they would not pick up because we were registered as spam. Ultimately, there was no contact and therefore there was no cold call.

An expert on sales would have probably told me how the key concept to take away from these three books is to understand that you will have to contact people who don't know you. When you reach out to those people, you should prepare yourself adequately. These experts may also add new techniques and software that could help me along that process as well.

The last advantage of speaking to experts is that you are now mixing and mingling with them. That does well for your social proofing and it would allow you to build relationships with high-level people within your field. That alone is worth your time and will prove beneficial in the long run through opportunities that are opened to you from being in the proximity of those currently doing better than you.

Rule No 3: Amazon

Amazon is the largest online store where books are sold digitally and physically.

There are 4 things you want to look at when you use Amazon as a research tool:

1. Market size
2. Reviews
3. Book cover layout
4. Price

In regards to the market size, I covered that in depth under Chapter 5 of the book. I would, therefore, like to engage you in the other three.

Let's start with reviews.

Reviews

This feedback is essential if you are looking to write a good book.

There are three types of reviews you want to look at. The first type is the one-star reviews. The one-star reviews resemble readers who are displeased with the content of the book. The book did not meet their expectations. On the horizon of one-star reviews lays a twofold opportunity for you. Firstly, they show you what you ought not to do and therefore they show you what you ought to do as well. Try to infuse both of those elements into your book.

Once you're done with the one-star reviews then have a look at the five-star reviews. The five-star reviews are where audiences have fallen deeply in love with the author's content. You want to make sure that most of your content is in alignment with that. If it's not, then maybe you could think about how you can begin to spruce up your content in such a way that people are going to enjoy it just as much as the reviews you are reading.

Lastly, you have three-star reviews. Three-star reviews are the most balanced for me. The five stars and the one-star are two extreme ends of a spectrum. The three-star reviews are right in the center of the two. You can learn constructively from these reviews due to their balanced nature. Once again you will know what to add and what to subtract within your content.

Remember that you have the ultimate choice as to whether or not you want to incorporate this into your book and to what degree as well. Whatever your choice, the ramifications are that it will affect the longevity of your book.

Book cover layout

Search for books that are in your genre. Have a careful look at what the covers of those books look like, especially the bestsellers. I would not advise you to mimic them but I would recommend that you see what you could incorporate from them. In my case, there seemed to be a pen or a writing object on most covers. I made the choice to follow suit but to express it in my own way.

I know you have heard that you should never judge a book by its cover - I am telling you to. The first thing anyone will do is judge your book cover. Subconsciously it would already tell them what to expect. I would advise you to be proactive by using this information to bolster you forward. It is actually said a book cover could cost you up to 30% of your sales or could increase them by that same margin. Isn't that worth taking advantage of?

As you look at the designs of other book covers, have a look at how the titles and subtitles are crafted. You will see a formula begin to unveil; once it has unveiled completely have a look to see how you can apply it to your title as well. I would still advocate that you find a balance between applying that formula and also ensuring that you don't sound like everyone else. Your unique voice and perspective are very important.

Price

Generally, on Amazon, self-published books sell for far less than traditional publishing houses. While it is the norm, I would still ask that you follow your logic and charge a price that you are most comfortable with.

On Amazon, you have the option to sell both a hardcopy and softcopy version of your book. As a rule of thumb, your hardcopy should be at least 20% more than that of your softcopy.

Offline of Amazon, however, I have been asked at our workshops whether there is a specific science to price, to which I honestly have found none.

I know people would validate the price of their book by how much of an investment they have made financially in their book. I believe at the foundation of this is the hope to ensure they make their investment back. If this is your strategy, I would rather you don't publish your book at all. It will only cause you heartache financially. To make the money back on your book merely through sales when starting out will put a huge amount of stress on you. I am not asking you to be frivolous with your spending in creating your book; I am, however, asking that you admit that you are trying things out and because of that you may win or you may lose. You, therefore, have to set your mind on what the goal of your book was. That is of far greater importance.

Another thing to note is that you do not make money from your book; rather you make money *because* of your book. Your job, especially if you are writing a nonfiction book, is to leverage your book to create services or products that people will buy with greater margins. Your book will, therefore, be used to social proof your self-image in the minds of your consumers and will enable you to easily obtain further finances from them. That should be your main focus.

The idea I would like you to, therefore, latch onto would be to rather take the investment into your book as a sunk cost and work towards how you would leverage the opportunity instead.

So, what should I charge then?

Charge what you believe your work is worth to you. I have had a book sold to me for R550 and books sold for R100. "All you ever need is one sale to validate you.", a client once mentioned to me. I agree and once you have made that initial sale, more will come trickling in if you have a good marketing plan in place.

You would obviously have to consider the fact that the higher the price the less likely it is people will buy from you and vice versa ceteris paribus. This is basic economics. What basic economics forgets is that ceteris paribus is the starting block to understanding this concept. We know in the real world outside of the class or lecture room you will have other determinants. The following are some of them:

1. **Income level of audience**
   The higher the income level the more you can charge. The less you charge in this environment the more likely that people will not buy from you. The converse is also true.

2. **Availability of other alternatives**
   Are there other books in your genre? If so, what they are charging may influence what you can charge too. Going above the price may lead people to not buy but also going below that price may do exactly the same thing.

   This would also apply to you if you are selling your book in a bookstore, at a book festival, or at an event where you will have other authors selling their books too. You may get away here with selling below everyone else, but there is no guarantee as people may think your product is inferior.

3. Advertising

The more you advertise the better your chance of selling because people can only buy what they can see. The better the advert from an aesthetic point of view, the more you could charge for your book.

If you are a speaker this can be as simple as letting the people attending know that your book will be on show.

4. Seasons

Check the seasons for when book sales do well. Depending on where you are from, they will vary. When you choose your price try to ensure that whatever the season you can still make decent sales.

For instance, selling a book during January and April may be a tad difficult in South Africa due to people in January recovering from spending in December. It may be in your best interest to then ensure that the price of your book caters to that. In April people are leaving for a holiday and thus book sales would probably be slow in terms of demand; ensure your book prices cater to that as well.

This is what I mean by there is no real science to setting a price for a book. There may be fundamentals to adhere to but the fundamentals become complicated when applied because you cannot truly guarantee the outcome.

Knowing that there is no guarantee I would advise that you stick to what you can control and letting go of the rest. In this case, you can control your price. So, set one that is fair to you. Whatever you charge just ensure you always know that your book will be judged because of it; it comes with the territory. The less you charge the more people may think the quality is of no good, the more you charge, however, the converse then applies. This is regardless of the fact of whether or not they actually purchase from you.

My last words pertaining to this are if you would like to charge a premium for your book make sure you look and sound the part. In the non-fiction publishing world, this is ensuring you are dressed formally, have a banner, and perhaps a speed point for purchases as well. If you are a speaker, ensure your slides are impeccable. All these small things will add up to how many copies you will sell.

There was a corporate speaking engagement that I was invited to with another speaker. I had my first book on me selling at R200. The other speaker brought their books as well; they had three on them, which totaled R400. All of his books where much larger than mine in size. Intimidated by what I thought the audience may say, I thought: "Shall I reduce my pricing, so that they don't complain?" Now not that I am crazy but a moment later I responded: "Grant, charge your price!" So, I stuck to my prices and decided not to budge if asked to.

While I did learn my lesson that having more books available is better, I could not stop imagining how much more the other speaker would have made had he just charged R200 per book. It would have been easily R600 per customer as opposed to R400. Deep inside, this broke my heart because I know the audience would have paid him at that price point. R200 extra, especially with a large audience, can add up. This is a huge opportunity cost when lost. Learn from both of us. Write multiple books but also charge a worthwhile fee for each of them.

The last lesson that engagement taught me is that, depending on the size of the audience, you may want to bring someone to accept payments for your books as you sign. It will ensure you get through your queues as fast as possible and it also makes you look more organized and important in the eyes of your buyers. Incentivize your salesperson and chances are they will get more copies signed for you. I have seen this personally work at events I have been invited to.

> ## QUICK QUESTION:
> How much will you charge for your book?

CONCLUSION

The success of your book will depend to a large extent on how much research you do. The research on the consumer you wish to serve, the content in your book, the cover of your book, and the pricing of your book as well.

The more in-depth knowledge you have of those points, the higher your chances of succeeding with the sales of your book.

THE LACK OF THE ENTREPRENEURIAL SPIRIT – HOW YOUR BOOK BECOMES YOUR BUSINESS CARD

"To succeed these days, authors must be more business-like than ever." – Schumpeter, The Economist

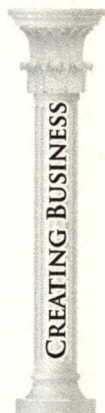

Figure 7 The Five Pillars of Self-Publishing © - Creating a Business

CHAPTER 19
WHAT IS A BUSINESS?

A business[11] by definition is a trade considered in terms of its volume or profitability.

What this essentially means is that as you look to become an Authorpreneur, you have to ensure you have a plan to become profitable. If not from the onset, then definitely in the short term of you selling your books as you begin to build services and products.

To create a profitable business, whether part or full time, it entails two important elements:

1. Sales
2. A system

Element Number 1: Sales

By definition, a sale is the exchange of a commodity for money. Your starting commodity will be your book. Everywhere you go, on every occasion you are brought to, you have to ensure that you have your book with you. This would

---

11   https://www.lexico.com/en/definition/business

naturally increase the likelihood of sales and therefore decrease the chance of your books gathering moths and dust in your garage.

Let me introduce you to an idea from my book *"The Golden Goose Masters the Art of Selling"*. The idea is entitled the *"Sales Wheel of Insight"*. This wheel will give you the basic framework to ensure you are able to transition prospects to leads, and then leads to sales.

The Sales Wheel of Insight is divided into 5 rings:

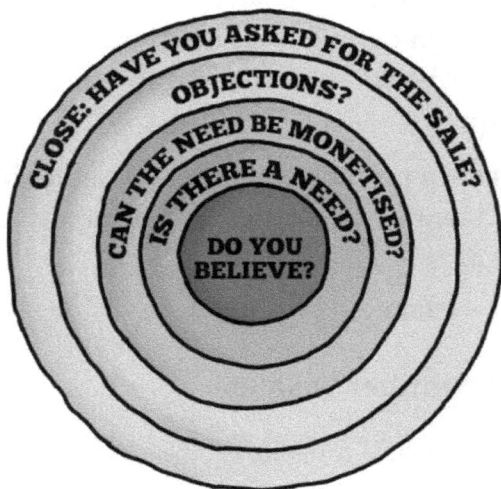

Figure 8 The Sales Wheel of Insight ©

I will only take you through the first three rings, as they are what are most applicable at this point in your journey.

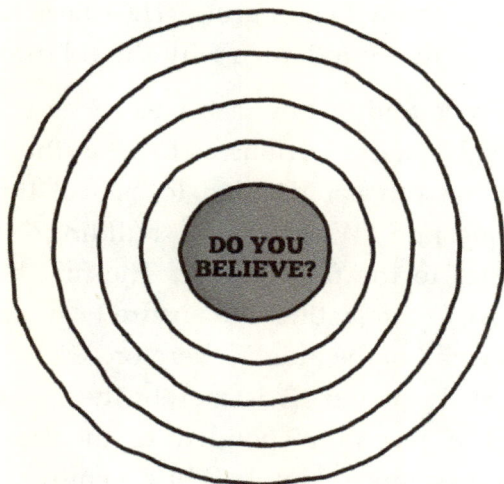

Figure 9 The Sales Wheel of Insight © Do you believe?

1. Do you believe?

I want you to deeply consider whether you believe in the fact that your book serves as a solution to someone.

I believe for anyone to sell something success-fully, there has to be a strong belief in what they are selling. My experience is that people tend to buy more from those who have a stronger conviction about their products and services. This does not mean you shout from rooftops or in malls, rather it means that people can see and feel your enthusiasm. Just think about it. When was the last time you bought something from someone who wasn't enthusiastic about their offering? The rule is simple: if you aren't interested, then why should they be?

A story is told of how a traveler was walking past three builders. Curious as to what they were building the traveler decided to ask all three of them a question "What are you building?" asked the traveler to the first builder. The first builder responded, "I am just here to ensure I can pay my bills at the end of the month, therefore what I build doesn't really matter. It is merely the fact that I build." The second responded to the traveler's question by saying, "I am building a church." And immediately went back to work. Lastly, the traveler asked the third builder. This builder looked into the traveler's eyes and said with enthusiasm, "I am building a place where people will connect with their Creator and their Creator with them." Same service different outlook. If you had the choice to hire one of these builders, which would it be? Become that builder.

I will be honest. I have not always been enthusiastic. I remember being at a Toastmasters meeting and one of the participants asking whether I had my book with me. I did. I, however, was very sluggish with my approach to giving it to her. That cost me. The enthusiasm she had greeted me with, I didn't return. Her body language went from "I want your book" to "Hmmm, perhaps next time". As you would guess next time never came. You may get bored of selling your book and that is human, don't however allow that to be shown to anyone who shows interest in your book. It may be your 100th time selling it but it's their first time buying it. Always keep that in mind.

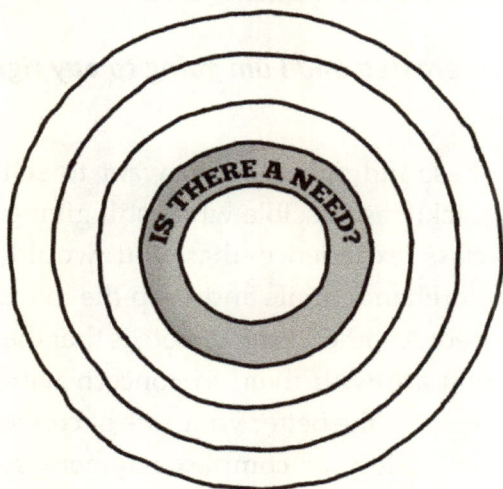

Figure 10 The Sales Wheel of Insight © Is there a need?

2. Is there a need?

Your Golden Thread and research should attest to this.

People pay to alleviate the need. If there is no need, then there is no sale. The clearer you are about your Golden Thread upfront and about what your books aim to solve, the easier it will be to communicate it to the prospects you meet with.

There are 4 sets of people that you will come across when you are selling your book. Your job is to recognize them and know how much attention you would want to allocate to them.

I am interested and I am going to buy right now...

With these individuals, you want to sell your book as quickly as possible while still giving them a world-class experience that you would have crafted beforehand. Smile and keep the interaction light-hearted. Another thing to note is that the more efficient you are with them in concern with your payment system, the better your rate of conversion. If you have a slow or complex payment system, people who were interested may decide otherwise and ask, "Perhaps next time?" We both know how that is likely to end.

Within the South African context, this means having your card machine, a printed and laminated QR code, and your cell phone number visibly displayed for instant bank payments.

Efficiency is the name of the game.

***I am interested and I want a conversation
with you before I buy your book...***

This group is interested but unlike the first group, they want to enquire a bit more about your book and perhaps get to know you better.

This is where you need to have mastered your Golden Thread and particularly how it would solve their needs. You are not pitching to them however, instead you are unraveling what their needs are and how you serve as a solution.

Depending on how that conversation goes they will either buy your book immediately, opt to buy it later, or they may not buy it at all.

Take no offense if they decide to buy it later or decide not to. Remember your book is meant to serve a need and therefore must land in the most deserving hands.

If this group of people decides to buy your book at a later stage ensure you know when they plan to make this purchase. Agree on a date. You and the buyer need to be clear on that otherwise it will be a tad difficult to convert their delayed decision to purchase into an actual sale. As you ask do not be pushy; instead, smile while being frank.

I am interested in and will buy your book later...

You have two options with this group, regardless of your choice however you need to ensure you take down their details so you can convert them later.

Here are your options:

1. After taking their details, figure out when they would want to secure the book. Then follow up with them by sharing a link with an online form where you have your banking details so that they can EFT you your book fees. Subsequently, you would then courier a signed copy to them.

    Your book in this scenario has not changed hands yet. This only will happen once you have seen proof of payment.

2. The second option entails you giving them the book and sending them an invoice for it. This will affect your cash flow if they do not pay on time. It, however, guarantees that you have one. Follow up with the following sentence: "Hi ... just following up, you haven't by any chance processed that payment as of, yet have you?" That sentence keeps face with your prospect and is usually followed up with: "Oh, sorry. I

will do so now." To which you will respond, "Thank you, do send me proof of payment once you have." If they do not tell you when they will make the payment then agree upon a date and follow up.

Just so you know, I have never had someone not pay for their book unless I felt they shouldn't. The longest I have had to wait for payment is 3 months. If you find yourself in a similar position, don't stop selling in wait for that payment. I would highly suggest you always keep selling during that period as you consistently follow up for your payment. You would want to keep incoming cash flow top of mind.

I am not interested and would not buy your book even if it was for free...

Leave these people alone. Do not try to convince them and do not try to pitch to them. You would be wasting your time and their time too. Also, take no offense to their disinterest. Remember that your book is meant to reach those in need of it. They are helping you with that process, be thankful and move right along to someone else.

As you sell your book, these people will not appear in an organized fashion, nor will they have stickers on their foreheads letting you know which category they fit in. You would just need to be alert and watch out for cues. I can guarantee you that the more you expose yourself to opportunities where you can sell your book, the sharper you will become in recognizing who belongs to what group. So, go out there and learn.

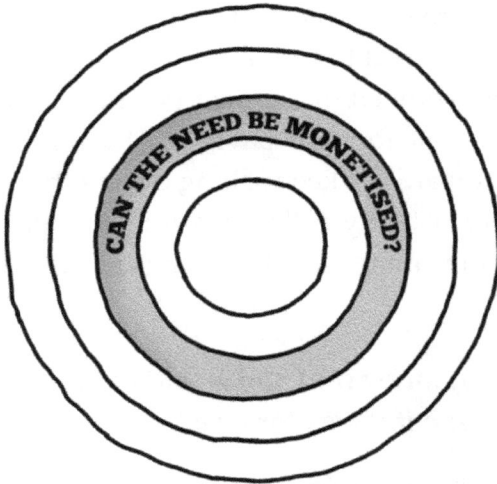

Figure 11 The Sales Wheel of Insight © Can the need be monetised?

3. Can the need be monetised?

If there is a need, then there should be a price to pay to alleviate your buyers' need. You should already have this price upfront. Whatever the price is, do not flinch when you mention it to a prospective buyer. Also do not state your price and then leave an awkward silence looming in the air. Rather follow up and close the transaction with the question, "To whom will I be signing this book to and will you only be buying one copy?" Always assume the affirmative.

We're still on the topic of creating a profitable business. If all the answers to the Sales Wheel of Insight are affirmative then it is time to work on your volume of sales. This speaks to your system.

Element Number 2: A system

A system[12] is simply an organized framework.

In the case of your business, it would be an organized framework of how you will sell your book as you begin to build other products and services that would ensure predictable sales.

As simplistic as that sounds, I can assure you that it is not that easy or quick. It will take time.

The system I used for my first book was getting to a gathering or event where I would be speaking, for which I would have built a keynote around my

---

12   https://www.lexico.com/en/definition/system

book, and after the keynote, I would sell copies of my book.

I would also announce on social media where I was going and that my book would be traveling with me. The fact that I could speak well and I kept announcing my whereabouts allowed me to consistently be selling.

The only problem with this system is that if I am not going anywhere on any certain day, then guess what? My book doesn't sell and therefore no income for that day.

Thus far I have been able to turn my books into an electronic format and sell them off Amazon. This has certainly helped the process and ensures that I am still selling my book without being physically present. I still make more sales directly but I am beginning to master how to sell on Amazon through short courses offered on the internet and the books I am reading on the subject matter too. The most helpful read has been Ray Brehm's *The Snowball Book Launch*[13]. Get it. You will love it.

I am also looking to partner up with Takealot, who already has a distribution channel.

---

13 https://www.amazon.com/Snowball-Book-Launch-Pre-Order-Self-Published-ebook/dp/B07JM9C2DM

I also want you to know upfront that your journey will be different from mine. So, aim to look for a system that serves you best as you model and modify mine.

> **QUICK QUESTION:**
> What type of system are you going to build?

On your journey to becoming an author, you would either start off as an expert or novice. Now, this is important because it will affect how you create your products and services.

CHAPTER 20
EXPERT VS NOVICE

There are two different starting points in an author's journey; you either start as a novice or an expert. Both of these individuals seek the credibility that becoming an author offers. The difference is how they are perceived by the market which they serve. By market I simply mean customers.

You will either fall into one of these categories. Neither is better than the other. The point is to be aware of your starting point. If you are an expert you will create your book by moving backward from your products and services. If, however, you are a novice then you would create your book by moving forward.

The expert

The expert is one who already has the experience of dealing with a captive audience and therefore has some sort of clientele already. These individuals are already credible due to the experience that they have had within the market place. When an expert becomes an author, it solidifies them further in the mind of their audiences and allows them to increase their pricing as well.

Experts work backward

The reason experts work backward is because they have already at this point created and sold products and services.

By publishing a book, they further solidify themselves as an expert in the minds of their clientele. Their books will usually compose of how they do business and what insights they have gathered over time. As they begin to give or sell books to their current client base, their clients will begin to deem them as more valuable. This also opens the doors for new clientele through the sale of their books. As a result of this new base to sell to, there is a promise of new leads developing.

I have a client who I am keeping accountable with their quota of words they are meant to reach on a weekly basis. She has been a transformational coach for about 20 years. The people she has helped through her coaching have been asking her to write a book. Once she has published it, she will further solidify herself as an expert in the minds of her current clientele. A further bonus is that her book would also generate new leads.

Are you an expert? What are you waiting for?

The novice

The author that is a novice to their market is only a novice because they are not yet known - even though they would have written a book and as a result have credibility in their subject matter. They may not be seen or treated as an expert yet. Real-life experience is still needed and that can only be developed with time. The credibility of writing and publishing a book, however, would open doors for a novice that would otherwise have been previously closed or very hard to enter.

Novices work forward

By forward I simply mean that after their book they would need to look at what products and services they could build based on the book that would serve their clientele.

This, however, is not an easy task because novices have an idea of what they would like to offer but don't necessarily know whether it will work or not.

If you fall in this bracket, I want you to acquaint yourself with one word: patience. You of all people will realize that what you may have started with may not be what people want from you. Instead, they may request other services that have nothing to do with your book at all. Do not be disheartened, instead, remain humble and listen. You are being led to a goldmine of opportunity.

I have had a client who has written a book on how to build inner strength. As we speak, she is currently mentoring and running workshops that equip young women on how to think big and form a plan to actualize their dreams. I mentioned to her that it is paramount she continues to serve those willing to invest in her services. As she serves their needs, the path to monetizing her offering will become as clear as day.

If you have a full-time job and you are a novice because I love you, I will tell you upfront: do not, I repeat, do not leave your job. Keep it and grow your business on the side. Remember what I said about patience? Your moment will come if you give yourself and your business some time.

My story

When I left my first job as a financial planner, for the first time in my life I saw financial hardships wash up on my shore.

In order to circumvent this, I decided to get back into the job market. Unfortunately, the only jobs that were available were in financial planning.

I knew I needed a different path and decided to write a book. As a novice, my book would give me credibility in becoming a professional speaker and life coach. Well, at least I thought. Upon publishing my book, the speaking and life coaching sessions were hard to come across.

Each time someone bought my book, I thought I would hear: "Do you do life coaching?" That request floods my gates now, but then it was not the case. Instead, I kept getting asked if I could help them publish their books. I refused initially and mentioned how that was not part of my expertise. Did the requests stop? No.

The number of requests kept growing, so I decided to create a seminar on how to write a book and self-publish within a year.

I want you to take note of something then I promise to get back to the story. You may not feel like an expert when asked to do something out of your scope and that's okay. If someone else views you like one, however, then that is what really matters. Repeat that to yourself over and over again because what novices are guilty of at times is thinking they have to see themselves the way other people see them. Not going to happen. If you wait for your confidence to reach that level, I can promise you that the river of opportunity will dry up and you will go thirsty.

Another idea to take heed of is that as a novice you are building two businesses. Firstly, you are building a business for the future. In my case, this was the life coaching and professional speaking business. Your first business will take time. As your first business is coming together, you need to build your second business. This is the business that is the bridge between where your business is currently and where it will be in the future. This bridge will give you experiences that will only aid your second business. Usually, the lessons learned here have small margins of error even though at the time you make them you will tend to make a mountain out of a molehill. Be humble during this time and build that second business while keeping your future business top of mind at all times. The reason you would want to keep your first business top of mind is that you could get so involved in the second business that you forget its purpose as a bridge. We get onto bridges to go to the next destination; we never make the bridge our final destination.

Now back to my story.

The seminar I put together was for 40 minutes. After it was done, I was surprised by the fact that people wanted more. Urged on by a very close friend of mine, Luyanda Dlamini, I designed a half-day workshop on how to write and publish a book.

After the workshops, delegates would want to know whether I could help keep them accountable by coaching them through the process. I agreed to do so and set up a service. This service allowed me to charge per 90-minute session I was with them. In those sessions, I help them from fleshing out their concept to finally getting their first manuscript completed.

It wasn't long until the clients I helped write their manuscript asked that I help them publish it into a book.

It then dawned on me that people saw me as an expert when it came to publishing and author coaching. I am glad for the likes of Luyanda who persisted that I develop something even though I felt I didn't want to. Her persistence allowed me to make the most of the river of opportunity that was coming my way. I now have taken full advantage of this river of opportunity by creating this book, to further identify me as an expert within this field.

Looking back at my journey, I can tell you that the most important thing as a novice looking forward is to ensure you listen to the market and what they want from you post your book launch.

Create what they desire and see how much more value you could add to them.

> **QUICK QUESTION:**
> Are you a novice or an expert?

As you would begin to pick up, I want you to build a business from your book. Let me share with you the reasons why in the next chapter.

CHAPTER 21
WHY START A BUSINESS FROM YOUR BOOK

I know not everyone who reads this book is entrepreneurial. Despite this fact, I would highly consider you take it upon yourself to try and formulate a business around your book for two reasons:

1. Income
2. Service

Income

You will make money from your book sales but you will make more money because of your book. Once you become an author you can leverage your credibility into selling other products and services which will sell for much more.

Another important point here is how this begins to constitute a new stream of income. Why not command and draw more?

A danger here, however, is becoming greedy. I have seen this happen in my journey. I just wanted more money and therefore would charge high amounts to my current clientele for other ad hoc services and forgot that the reason any business stays alive is that they are serving a need.

As long as you are serving a need and your focus is on that wholeheartedly and honestly, the money will come. Over time I have learned to put the needs of my clients consistently before that of mine. This has also meant not getting paid for services that I could have been paid for just to be of service. Just so we are clear when I say client, I mean someone that has agreed will pay your price. I am not referring to a prospect that is still making that decision. The free services I gave were entirely out of a heart of gratitude, it was not to onboard them to another of my other services.

Another reason you do not want to make this about the money is that once you do, you will never be satisfied with how much you are making. Now while not being content is a good trait to have in business, it does not always translate well for your client. I don't know about you but I don't feel comfortable when I can tell the person I am speaking to simply cares about their bottom line and not solving for my need. Do not fall into that trap. Instead, lead with love by ensuring your customers' needs are met first. Yours will be met next. Let go of all expectations and give whole-heartedly. It will come back to you.

Service

Your book is going to serve a need by being a solution to someone's problem. This, however, is the start of your journey because if your reader resonates with your material then they would want more from you. There are about 20 services or products you can create from a book.

Before I share them with you, I would advise as you look through the list that you focus on three at the beginning and then work yourself up to doing more. Also, keep an ear out to what your clients may ask of you.

Here is the list of products and services you could create and get paid for:

1. Your actual book.
2. The audio version of your book.
3. The e-book version of your book.
4. A curriculum.
5. A workbook.
6. A keynote.
7. A tour.

8. A workshop.
9. A course.
10. Consultation services.
11. A coaching program.
12. A mastermind group.
13. A paid community.
14. A paid webinar.
15. Paid conference calls.
16. Seminars.
17. Screenplays.
18. A movie.
19. Merchandise.
20. Apparel.

Something to note about these 20 products and services is that how you create them is dependent on 2 things.

1. What you believe would be best aligned to your book as and while you are writing it, or after you have written the book.
2. What your clients would ask of you.

If you care for the audience deeply and believe you hold the solution to what keeps them up at night then creating the above products and services is imperative. You creating them will ensure that you are perpetually helpful and a source of empowerment to your client base.

It is also a win-win situation because you get to serve and not go hungry because of it.

QUICK QUESTION:
Are you going to start a company?

So, what are you going to do with all the money you will be making from your book?

CHAPTER 22
WHAT TO DO WITH THE MONEY?

You are going to start receiving some money for your book and I think it is important that you know what to do with the money upfront. You have the following four options:

1. Reinvest
2. Create another book
3. Create another product or service
4. Give copies away

Reinvest

Always ensure that you have copies of your book on you at all times. This is non-negotiable. Not having your book on you would be a sure way of forfeiting income. The statement usually shared is "Cash is king"; personally, however, I believe "Cash today, is king".

Create another book

Every book published is never complete. There is always something that the author would have wanted to share with the audience but never got the chance to due to various reasons.

You are not exempt from this feeling. You will see what I mean soon enough. You could also co-author a book.

The other importance of this is that it allows you to remain relevant and active in the eyes of your audience. It will also begin to open another stream of income and the various opportunities that the book would present.

I had a chat with a lady who owns a book store. Her advice to me was that as a self-published author, you truly begin to realize financial returns after your third book. Need I say more?

Create another product or service

After the release of my first book, I got requests to help aspiring authors to make their aspirations come to life.

I took some of the proceeds from my first book and began running workshops. This worked out very well for me.

Just a word of caution that when you do this ensure that whatever you create is a result of a demand from your audience. This will guarantee the likelihood of more sales than if you were to guess on their behalf.

Give copies away

There will be a time when you will give copies of your book away. This is how a book turns into a business card. It is however very dependent on who you give it to and why.

Ensure you give your book over to someone who has the authority to buy more copies from you. Whether they do or do not is not imperative, what is imperative is ensuring there is the possibility of this happening. I know off the bat that may sound selfish, remember however that your book is like a seed in this scenario. You want to plant your seed in the right soil from the onset. So rather than selfish, you are being cautious.

To further etch yourself in the minds of those whom you give your book to ensure you follow up with communication and how you may be of assistance to them in the future. This would increase the likelihood of striking a deal. Consistency will ensure this becomes a reality.

Let me quickly share with you how it has worked on me.

There was a pageant where I was asked to be the master of ceremonies. At this pageant, I met up with a young lady called Megan who was one of the participants. Megan at the tender age of 15 is already an author.

She gave me a signed copy of her book at her pageant. I appreciated the gesture. Ever since that point in time, she has always been on my mind. If ever there is a speaking engagement and the audience is primarily composed of teenagers guess who I'm going to call? Megan! She leveraged the opportunity and now her book will serve her as a perpetual business card.

Take the lead from Megan and plant those seeds. Do not however fall into the trap of waiting for *how* something will happen. Let go of all the expectations of *how* and know for a fact that something *will* come around someday. It always does.

QUICK QUESTION:
What will you do with the money you receive from your book?

I have alluded to it time and time again, but I really want to hone in on the patience you need in this process. Let me enlighten, equip, and empower you by asking you to turn the page once more.

CHAPTER 23
BE PATIENT

Wealth vs money

In Njabulo Nkosi's second book[14] he eloquently shares how we ought to look at ourselves as a business because we are.

One of the chapters I thoroughly enjoyed was a chapter on wealth vs money. Money, as argued by Njabulo, is simply a numerical measurement of wealth. You obtain money from providing a service or product that the buyer would find value from and in exchange will give you their money for it.

Wealth, on the other hand, is a system you create to allow money to flow.

In publishing a book, you have developed a system that will allow money to follow in your direction. It is imperative that you be patient and not view your published book as a get-rich-quick

---

14 You are a Business, Treat Yourself Like One: The 5 Essentials for Personal Transformation and Building a Better Future!

scheme. It's not. It is only the entrance leading you to wealth.

While you would have now developed a system to allow money to flow in your direction, your next job is to ensure that you gain maximum flow and that takes time and market feedback.

The saying goes: "Good things may come to those who wait but great things come to those that hustle." I believe that to the person that can do both wait and hustle, ginormous things are on their way. Learn to do both, by doing the work necessary but detaching yourself from how the outcome will come about.

QUICK QUESTION:
How will you remain patient as you
build your business from your book?

Okay, so where do you start once you have published your book?

CHAPTER 24
WHAT TO DO AFTER PUBLISHING YOUR BOOK

What social media platforms will you use to keep in contact with your audience?

I will go in-depth a tad later concerning this during the marketing phase of this book. For here and now though, something I have picked up on and continue to when I read other books on publishing or marketing is that you need to keep communicating with your audience. No communication, no business.

So upfront, I would want you to pick a way you are going to keep in contact with your audience and how frequently you would want to do so. Communication is the lifeline of your business.

As a financial planner, we would sell insurance and investment products and services. One of the things my manager would keep reminding me was to continuously stay top of mind with all my clients because once they have bought from you, they will continuously buy if you remain relevant in their lives. How do you remain relevant? Communication.

This is why some authors will ask for your email address and send you an email frequently. This is also why authors will set up blogs or YouTube channels. Communication.

Book fairs

While I was waiting for my first book to come in from the printers, the idea came to me to enter my book into book festivals.

I must have emailed at least 15 to 20 book festivals and only 1 came back to me. It was a lucky break for me because this put me in front of another audience that had not heard from or of me before.

I would recommend the same thing. Have a look at your local or international festivals and give yourself a shot at getting onto other platforms.

I would advise that it is not just about being in the presence of a new audience. It is also about ensuring you have a means to consistently chat with them as well. So do prepare adequately by having your backend communications highlighted and ready to communicate to anyone who shows further interest in your book or in you.

Having other products and services would aid you very well. Mention it casually however and not with the intention to make a sale immediately.

While at a book festival, depending on the format, if you are interviewed in front of an audience, find ways to make them laugh. I am not too sure why, but people are more likely to buy when you have a sense of humor. People seem to connect more with that.

Broadcasting opportunities

Getting onto your local radio or television shows would also allow you to begin to get better coverage of your book.

To ensure that broadcasters give you airtime, I would advise that you do some homework around what programs they normally host during the year and how your book would enable them to add more value to their programming.

Believe it or not, this is more in arms reach than we are made to believe. Broadcasters are always looking for new content. Make it your duty to get it to them.

I recently was able to get onto a television show and as a result, I could add that incredible logo:

"AS SEEN ON TV". Needless to say, this has given more gusto to my first book.

All the opportunities that I am sharing with you just ensure your book remains relevant and gives it the chance to land in new hands. You have to keep doing this until you get to the point that you feel the market has been saturated. Will it ever? I highly doubt it. Remember there are millions of people that are out there and they will latch onto your book in their own space and time. So, keep putting yourself out there.

Book stores

I am not the largest fan of book stores. I will be upfront with that, but I do understand the positive impact they could have on one's credibility.

At a network meeting I was at, I met with a book distributor that said: "It is the dream of every author to see their books in a bookstore." I don't necessarily think this is true. I think the underlying need here is the distribution of an author's book. We as authors express that need as, "I need to be in a book store", but do you really need to be? I highly doubt it.

If that is your dream however there is nothing wrong with it. I would have to warn you, though, that if you are seeking validation from being in a store then you are not going about this the right way. Validation is forever thirsty. It never gets quenched. Once your book is in a store, then your next job would be to get it sold. After getting it sold it will be about becoming a bestseller. That ladder is never-ending and ever tiring. My best advice to you is to know why you are putting your book in a store and have a plan as to how you will get people into that book store as well.

Also, ensure you understand what the margins are. Some stores take up to 90% of the retail price of your book, so money is not one of the reasons you want your book in a store.

My largest reason against bookstores has always been the fact that once a reader comes into a store, your book needs to compete with all of the books inside that bookstore without you being there. Also, if your book does not sell, then your copies must leave the bookstore they are currently taking shelf life in. This means more stock for you to handle. This stock would have to find new ways of getting to people.

As a company, we upload our client's books onto Amazon and I know you are thinking, "Isn't that a bookstore Grant?" It is a bookstore. The similarity is that I would have to aggressively compete with other authors. The difference, however, is that I do not pay anything to have my book there and if someone would want a hardcopy of my book, guess what? Amazon will print it and get it to them without me having to finance anything. From a cost perspective, Amazon is a great bet.

I do see one advantage of having your book in a bookstore though: credibility. There is something about telling someone how they can find your book in a bookstore. Is it worth it, however? I will leave that answer up to you.

If you do decide to put your book in a bookstore after all my advice, please ensure you understand the agreements that the bookstore puts in place. Understand what your needs are and articulate them in such a manner that would make both yourself and the bookstore's partnership a success. Good luck.

QUICK QUESTION:
How will you expose your book to more people?

CONCLUSION

You can create a business from your book and you should. It will guarantee you more income and ensure that you are serving your client base for the long term as well.

For your business to form, it must be a solution to a need. This solution will be birthed from your audience who will give you hints on what else you could create. It will come from your Golden Thread and the consistent exposure of your book on social media or broadcast outlets.

Lastly, be patient as you begin to build your empire because you are creating wealth and wealth is not an overnight activity. It takes time.

Now for the last piece of this puzzle that will ensure you succeed in the game of self-publishing. It's time to market your book to the world, and I will share with you the plan. It's all waiting for you in the next and last section of this book.

LACK OF MARKETING – HOW TO DEVELOP A BRAND AND MARKETING PLAN FOR YOUR BOOK

"Marketing is really just about sharing your passion."
– Michael Hyatt

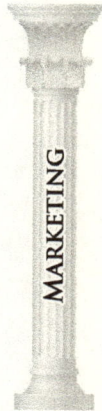

Figure 12 The Five Pillars of Self-Publishing © - Marketing

CHAPTER 25
BRANDING

What's a brand? A singular idea or concept that you own inside the mind of the prospect[15].

Do you know you are building a brand through your book?

Brand building through Authorpreneurship

I have heavily slanted developing a business around your book. I hope that as you have transitioned from page to page, you have already started thinking of company names you could register for yourself. This is advice that we give all our clientele. Start a business and build its foundation on your literary work.

One smart way of also going about this is to begin a series of books as opposed to a standalone book. Think of Robert Kiyosaki's "Rich Dad Poor Dad Series", Douglas Kruger's "50 Ways to...",

---

15 Ries, Al. The 22 Immutable Laws of Branding. HarperCollins e-books. Kindle Edition.

Richard Templar's "Rules of...", and my "The Golden Goose Series". With every book published in a series, you etch your branding further in the minds of your readers.

A series could also cause readers to buy and read the other books in your series if they resonate with the copy that they would have initially bought.

This is obviously challenging for the onset. I would further add that it should be. The point is not to get strung up on trying to figure everything out up front. Start with your first book, gain some experience and then move on to your next book and keep working through it bit by bit and the series will come to you.

If you decide to force a series, from the plethora of books I have read, the only difference between your books will be their covers. The content will most likely be the same. To not fall into that trap, live a little and go build experience. Journal everything and in due course, you will have a series that will add a lot of value to your leadership.

Your brand is everything about you

A friend of mine, Papi Fhatuwani Lidovho, gave me some profound advice months before my first book launch. He mentioned to me how everything

I wear and the ambiance I set in the room will speak towards my brand. He also cautioned how from here on out I have to be intentional about how I dress and share my story to further etch my brand in the minds of my audience. He was and to this day still is right.

Once you have branded yourself in a specific manner, does it mean that you can never change? That you are to remain with your brand image forever? No. You can change and there is no harm in that provided it isn't done too frequently. The change should also be purposeful.

Tips on branding

As you build your brand, I want you to take the following 3 things that I learned from '*The 22 Immutable Laws of Branding*' by Al and Laura Ries - a good buy if you would like further information on branding. Out of the 22 Laws, these were my favorite:

1. **The Law of Contraction: "A brand becomes stronger when you narrow its focus"**
    Ensure that whatever you offer to your clientele is focused. You do not want to be all over the show. The narrower your focus is, the more depth that you can offer. The greater the depth the more valuable you become.

If you are an expert in your field and you are interested in writing a book, this will be simple for you. For novices, naturally, this will be challenging from the onset because you are still trying to find your feet. I would suggest over time you finally get into spaces where you begin to narrow your services and products so that you can add depth as well.

2. **The Law of The Word: "A brand should strive to own a word in the mind of the consumer"**

As you build your brand, ensure you have one word in mind that you would like your audience to know you for. My word was "Potential" now I am looking to rebrand it to "Entelechy" which is the realization of potential. It may take time but I know it will be worthwhile for my future endeavors.

You will need one word too. What will it be?

3. **The Law of Advertising: "Once born, a brand needs advertising to stay healthy"**

If possible, from the onset ensure that you have a budget for advertising. Your advertising could be over the internet via Google Ads or any social media platform that allows for paid advertisements. It could also be in the form of banners and other physical material.

Here is the twist, however. The point of advertising is to keep your primary audience knowing that you exist more than ensuring you obtain a different audience. Those who do not advertise lose their market share to their audience. Keep advertising.

I know that may seem extreme for just a book but that is where your journey begins. Habits you practice at the start will seep into the rest of your journey. Why not start with good habits from the onset?

What comes first, branding or marketing?

Your branding always comes first. You have to know what you are engraving in the mind of your prospects, leads, or customers before you publicize it through your marketing methods.

Marketing[16] comes second because it speaks to the business process of creating relationships with customers and satisfying them. It would be hard to create a relationship and satisfy it if you don't know what you would like your audience, whether prospect, lead, or customer, to think about you.

So, before you go out and begin creating relationships, ask the question: "What I would want people to associate me with?"

---

16 https://en.wikipedia.org/wiki/Marketing

Branding by itself is null and void if you do not combine it with marketing. What is marketing? I'm glad you asked.

CHAPTER 26
MARKETING

Marketing is not...

1. *Selling*
2. *A once-off action*

Marketing is not selling

Marketing is not selling; those two are co-dependent actions but are different in and of themselves.

While marketing is seen as how you plan on creating relationships with and satisfying customers, selling is exchanging the value you have for the money your prospect has.

The better your marketing, the easier it is to sell. The better your sales strategy the easier your marketing will be.

Both of those work in tandem and for the sake of simplicity, we will put marketing before sales.

The formulae now forming in your mind should be branding, marketing, and then sales.

This formula expressed in the diagram below that I have entitled "The Cycle of Business Presence©", as described below:

Figure 13 The Cycle of Business Presence ©

Marketing is not a once-off action

Marketing is not a once-off action. Marketing demands your consistency. You have to ensure that your brand is consistently in the ears and eyes of prospects. So that one post you posted on Facebook and never posted again? You were not marketing, you were notifying.

A book I recently read entitled, *Creative Writing and Authorpreneurship* [17] and authored by Michael Flowers, states how once you have written a book you have to market it at least 20 minutes daily. I agree and further state that books do not fly off counters if people don't know about them. It is a purchase that people rarely feel guilty about because we have all been conditioned to believe that books are an investment. Let people know of the investment you have diligently prepared for them. If your books are in your garage, it is not due to no need, it is due to lack of marketing.

QUICK QUESTION:
What is marketing?

We have just covered the definition of marketing. Now I would like to share with you how to build a masterful marketing plan.

---

[17] https://www.amazon.com/Creative-Writing-Authorpreneurship-Michael-Flowers-ebook/dp/B008Y0JBQC

CHAPTER 27
THE ONE-PAGE MARKETING PLAN

I read avidly and out of all the marketing books that I have read, the *One-Page Marketing Plan*[18] authored by Allan Dib stands supreme. It is the most actionable and concise plan to date.

I am going to share his concept with you, immersed with my own experience of it. I also want you to know that although I am sharing this with you with a specific focus on your book, it will also work well with the products and services you will be creating as well.

If you are a novice, this information will feel like much but I can assure you it will benefit you tremendously. If you are an expert, however, then this section will just be a matter of strengthening what you are already doing well while hampering down on your weakness.

---

18 https://www.amazon.com/gp/product/B01B35M3SM

The One Page Marketing Plan breaks down a customer into three phases:

1. Prospect
2. Lead
3. Customer

Within those phases, there are 3 activities that you would be challenged to engage in order to turn your marketing plan into a reality. As we go through the steps, I want you to begin to look at your book, whether you are currently writing or about to begin.

Prospect

A prospect by definition is a person regarded as likely to succeed as a potential customer. A customer is someone who buys goods or services from a shop or a business.

In our world, as authors, a prospect is someone most likely to buy your book.

As first-time authors, who are still novices at your craft; this may be difficult to map out from the onset because the truth is that you really do not know who your ideal prospect is. If you are an expert in your field then you already know who your ideal prospect is and where you would find them too.

My target market

If you are a first-time author and novice, then your target market is anyone that answers to the solution that you possess within your Golden Thread. Your job as a first-time author is just to ensure that you begin to get vigilant with the type of people that are consistently buying your book and what else they would need from you.

For experts, your job is simpler because you would have had experience and you would know who your target market is.

Once you are done with writing out your target market, the next step is to figure out what your message to them will be.

My message to my target audience

For first time authors and novices, this is the part where you begin to look at the causes of the problem you want to solve and the solutions that you have. You would then use those causes and solutions to ensure that you begin to develop your messages to the prospects you believe would want to hear them.

The secret here, however, is that you want your messages to begin as questions as opposed to statements. Questions engage and demand a response.

An example of this would be in my case where the problem I wish to solve is ensuring more authors self-publish their work in less than a year. One of the reasons this does not happen is that people do not know what to write about.

My message to my target audience would be:

Alternatively, I could also just ask, "If you were to write a book, what would you write about and why?"

If you are an expert in your field then you should know how to craft the above already.

Once you have formulated your message to your prospect, you have to decide as to which media you will use to communicate to your target audience.

The media I will use to reach my target market

If you do not know the medium to connect with your audience, then perhaps some research would be needed here.

The reason for this particular step is that you need to reach your readers where they are as opposed to where you are.

You could reach them via social media, podcasts, videos, blogs, vlogs, or vlog casts.

There are a plethora of ways and your job is to hone in on what is effective.

Whatever media you use, just be sure to be consistent with your messaging. Consistency is king and will gain you a plethora of followers over time.

If you are not too sure where to reach your audience then start with the media you use.

The above three steps are for prospects. Prospects would be the largest portion of your funnel for sales.

Once a prospect is interested, they then turn from prospect to lead.

QUICK QUESTION:
Who is your prospect and how will you reach them?

The first segment of this plan shows you how to build prospects. How do you turn a prospect into a lead though? The next chapter discusses that.

CHAPTER 28
LEADS

A lead is someone who has shown interest in liking your book, product, or service and now would want to find out what the next step would be.

In your sales funnel, this is smaller than your prospect pool but larger than the sales you will actually make.

There are three steps you would need to master in order to transition from prospect to lead. They are as follows:

1. Your Lead Capturing System
2. Your Lead Nurturing System
3. Your Sales Conversion Strategy

1. Your lead capturing system

You would want to create a lead database that will ensure that you are in consistent contact with your leads.

Now there are two types of leads that you are going to be dealing with. It will sound familiar to what was discussed in the business section of this book, but the context and actions associated are completely different.

The first group of leads is interested in buying your book right now. The second group of leads is interested but not right now.

Take note that I did not add anyone that is not interested because they would have not filtered through from the prospect level. Everyone that engages with you at this point is interested.

To take full advantage of this, create a list. That list could be via a WhatsApp group, it could be via a web-based email marketing service or your emailing account.

Whatever your choice is, you want to ensure that every one that is part and parcel of that group has joined by their own free will or they knew you were going to add them. Do not add people without their permission.

Once you have picked a system and have figured out how interested parties can join that list, then you would move onto the next step.

2. Your lead nurturing system

Communication is the lifeblood of any business and your leads would want to hear from you on a regular basis.

Will you be writing to your leads in the form of a blog or newsletter? Perhaps it will be through audio via podcasting on various platforms? Maybe it will be through videos on YouTube or any other platform?

Whatever your choice, as stated before consistency is king when you communicate with your audience.

We treasure consistency so much because of the discipline that is needed to keep that up. This is why athletes are revered and placed on high pedestals.

A client of mine does this phenomenally. From Monday to Friday, every morning she sends a spiritual message to her audience to uplift them. She has done this for so long that the members she has on her list have formed lists of their own and send her broadcast to those lists.

When she released her book, naturally the audience was waiting and ready to buy. Consistency here was her ally and it can be yours too.

Nurturing your leads is really for the leads that are interested but for some odd reason do not want to buy your book just yet.

For the leads that are ready right now and would want to purchase your book, you will need a sales conversion strategy. You could use the same sales conversion strategy for the other two types of leads when they are ready to make a purchase too.

An important point to note here is that once someone has bought your book, they can still become a lead for another of your products. That is why you ought to keep the nurturing running perpetually.

3. Your sales conversion strategy

How will you convert that all into book sales? How will you transfer their money into your bank account?

It's actually very simple. I ask all aspiring authors to make use of Google sheets, an invoicing system, and a pay point machine.

Google sheets allow you to create a one-pager where you can ask for your client's details as well as give them access to your bank account for transfers. This is specifically helpful when your database is largely online.

The secret in making this work, however, is consistent follow-up. It's not that your leads are not interested in buying your book or that they are now stalling you. Most times, other things may take hold of their attention and push you further back down the line of importance. Keep reminding them.

One way I do this is via a phone call or I send reminders with the invoicing system that I have.

If, however, your buyer is right in front of you, have your pay point charged and ready to accept card payments. This is not negotiable. Most people will have their cards on them but chances are they will not have their money on them. Having a card machine on you, that you have practiced with to ensure a quick and effective payment, will ensure that you get those extra sales as opposed to, "You know what, let me get your book the next time you see me." Leads that say this are being honest, but I assure you that their interest would have waned. Missing sales opportunities like this I view as close to illegal, so have your pay point machine with you at all times. It should be fully charged too.

> **QUICK QUESTION:**
> How are you capturing your leads?

Now you would think that after they have purchased your book you are done with them, right?

Wrong! Now it is time for some after-sales service to ensure your new customer keeps buying from you.

CHAPTER 29
CUSTOMERS

There are three things you do when you have a customer. The purpose of these actions is based on the premise that once someone has bought from you, the chances that they will buy again will be very high.

The problem is that we do not keep in consistent communication with our customers and do not allow them to know that we still exist and we are ready and willing to serve them with the rest of our catalog.

When as authors we eventually have another book, guess what we do: "Hey, I have another book out. Would you be interested in buying it?" By this time your customer would have turned back into a prospect and that is another 6-step process to get them to buy again. How about you follow the next three steps and ensure that your customer remains a customer for life?

Here are the three steps:

1. Deliver a world-class experience
2. Increase the customer lifetime value
3. Orchestrate and stimulate referrals

1. Deliver a world-class experience

There is a famous man who had the world turned over from his dancing and singing. I am sure you have heard of him. Michael Jackson?

Michael Jackson could have just gone on the stage, and sang. Him just singing would have been a great job on its own. He could have also just danced; I am sure that would have been enjoyable too.

What did Michael do, however? He created experiences. He would touch his hat at a performance he was doing and that would excite the crowd. He would then lift his hand, covered by a shiny glove, and that would cause the crowd to scream endlessly. Then he would pause and by the time he had started singing some of his audience members would have fainted.

With your book, you need to plan on delivering or supplying it to your audience to create that effect. You want to make your leads not buy for the sake of buying; you want them to share an experience with you and thereafter tell everyone they know about it.

I have done this in two ways. Firstly, I have made sure I sign your book but not with just any type of message. Instead, I ask my leads about their 10-year goal. Once I know what that is, I sign their book congratulating them on obtaining it. Each time they read that, they are reminded of the goal that is ahead of them and that they have what it takes to complete it.

The second thing I do is to ensure that I have my customer's books in a gift bag with their name on it.

The dedication that I would give to this process would get my customers to ask what else I could offer them. This leads to more business.

That is the value of delivering a world-class experience time and time again. It creates raving customers that want more from you. Which then seeps into our next topic: what is the customer lifetime value?

2. Increase the customer lifetime value

As soon as you have sold something to a customer you have two choices:

1. Find more clients
2. Keep in constant communication with your current clientele database

I will not tell you which to focus on, what I will suggest is that you look at it from the point of view of how you can do both consistently.

Finding more clients to sell your book to is wise, but only doing this time and time again will lead you to a dead-end soon enough. Not to mention how tiring this can become.

You could also sell to a few customers and simply keep the ones that you have happy and that would mean eventually your pipeline runs dry. Your current customers can only buy so much from you.

A mix of both, however, is a primer for success. You should keep hunting for new sales but ensure that you are taking care of the ones that you currently have. Ultimately this means you never become desperate and you always have raving customers. If you can do this, your business will inevitably grow.

Through this two-fold approach, you will earn a lot but if you want more, the key is to orchestrate referrals.

3. Orchestrate and stimulate referrals

Your clients are your best salespeople, and they are willing to help you into their networks. Here is the catch, you have to ask.

The problem most of the time is that we never ask, but we lay there in deep expectation. Your expectation can only be met by communicating it.

Remember that referrals that come your way are already 80% closed. They will usually just want to see if the proof is in the pudding. If you show them the same respect and care that you gave their referee then you may have yourself a deal. It may not always translate into a sale but remember that is when you put them onto a list and feed them into your cycle.

Remember without the chance of referrals, you will find this journey very tough.

Testimonials

On a side note, another way to stimulate business is to ask your client base for testimonials about your book. Ask them to either send you a video, email, or a post on social media. This will only spur on more people to buy your book.

Use those testimonials in your sales copy when you advertise your book and the world will be at your feet.

If friends and family of the person who sent you a testimonial see that specific testimonial, chances are those friends and family will soon come your way too.

QUICK QUESTION:
How will you create raving fans that will happily dish you with referrals?

CONCLUSION

All the above will ensure that you are noticed and that your book will sell really well because you would have developed a systemized way to transition your clientele from prospects to leads, and then finally to raving customers who will give you referrals.

The more you repeat the above steps, the better you will become at fine-tuning this process. This will result in you knowing how to get great results with less effort.

Go out and market your book, the world is waiting.

IN CONCLUSION

In one of my keynotes, "From Hope to Belief and Finally to Faith – Three Elements that Build the Foundation to Entelechy", I highlight that for a dream to be realized, you need hope, you need belief, and you need faith.

Hope is simply the awareness that there is more out there waiting for you. In your case, it is the dream of becoming an author. Hope is a great starting point but after some time it is not enough. You need to have hope turn into belief. You have to believe that you can become an author.

Believing is based on understanding the systems that can turn your dream into actionable steps. Without a system in place that you can model and modify, you are doomed to make mistakes that will cost you a lot of money and time. It is therefore in your best interest to look for a system. I believe like many others that have gone through our company's processes that this book will be a beneficial system for you. Model and then modify it to your liking.

Belief, however, does run its course because while having a system is great, you have to work it. Without acting, belief can never translate into reality. This is where faith is birthed. Faith is acting on a set of steps without seeing the end process but knowing there is a system in place that will allow you to get to your goal. Your job is to work until you have obtained your desired results. Your job is to keep your faith burning until what is in your mind is finally in the world.

I may have never met you but I will tell you this much, if you have gone through this book then you have ticked off the hope and belief in becoming an author. Now find the faith to begin your journey. I have faith in you and I look forward to hearing about your book.

QUICK QUESTION:
When is your book launch date?

ABOUT THE AUTHOR

Grant Senzani strongly believes in your potential and how you can actualize anything and everything you desire to become. His mantra is, "We honour the dream, by doing the work".

He is a Distinguished Toastmaster, professional speaker, author of three books, and a certified life and body coach. He is also a certified neuro-linguistic practitioner.

He shares easy, yet very productive ways on how to become a successful self-published author.

If you or your team is looking to finally publish a book, then I would advise you to book him and his team by emailing info@thegoldengooseinstitute.com.

Our company also has a Facebook group entirely dedicated to you and authors like you on the same journey. Why not join others like you? The name of the group is The Golden Goose Becomes an Authorpreneur. Here is the link to it https://www.facebook.com/groups/534410874160599

Grant looks forward to hearing from you and being of service to you too.

REVIEWS

For the record, the reviews I am about to share with you are all from fellow authors, clients, or individuals that attended our workshops.

"It takes a great deal of courage to write and share your first book with the world. It takes a lot of love to have your second book be a gift to all aspiring authors. One may imagine that being an author would be a lonely journey but Grant has shown how it need not be. This book is a gem as it not only empowers you to start writing your own book, but it challenges you to create multiple income streams through the additional value you can offer to your readers. It is not just about becoming an author – it is about becoming an Authorpreneur."

Luyanda Dlamini
– Author of "What Had Happened Was..."

"I love the fact that the Author experienced what he is writing about. This book is well-researched and easy to apply."

Kirsty Adams
– Aspiring Author

"I thoroughly enjoyed reading this book. After following its guidance, I now know how my unborn book will be given birth to. I also enjoyed the fact that this book is easy to read and understand."

Gadifele Moeng
– Entrepreneur and aspiring author

"In this book, I have found a brilliant overview of how to uncover your potential as an aspiring author. In addition to this, it is a good reminder to stay focused if you already believe you are walking in your purpose.

"You would be surprised at how helpful people really are if you find the courage to ask." It's not always easy to put yourself out there, especially when you are on a journey of self -discovery. This book nudges you towards that nagging feeling that asks the question, "Am I enough?""

Cindy Jacobs
– Pastor and Author of "Changing Perspectives Everyday"

"The point that this book is not about becoming just an author, but an Authorpreneur is a hallmark. *The Golden Goose becomes an Authorpreneur* presents an applicable and yet valuable business strategy to transit your writing aspirations into a success."

Sir Mpho. M
– CEO of EmporeCorp and Author of "EMPOWERED TO PERFORM"

"The book is very insightful in how it articulates the key foundations of authorship. However, it also takes it a step further by embodying the entrepreneurship of turning your work into a business. Fantastic!"

Buntu Majaja
– Founder of DUYO, Director at SA Innovation Summit and Author of "Starting Your Start-Up in 90 Days"

"Are you faced with various questions, doubts, and fears about becoming an author? Then, search no more! This book is the most informative, uncomplicated and humorous, yet extraordinary guide, to assist upcoming authors, to realize their dream of becoming an Author.

I applaud the way the author is able to personify two of the most crippling emotions namely, doubt and fear, and teaches you how to use them to your advantage. This book will definitely motivate you to understand and believe, as Grant says, that "You may not start out capable and that's fine, but you should know that, you will end capable". And this assurance, no other book has been able to give me.

Thank you, Grant Senzani, for not only enabling me to become an author but to become a successful one at that."

Advocate Jenilee Daniels
– Aspiring Author

"Grant is the epitome of success and this is easily one of the essential books every aspiring author should read if they are looking for proven and honest hacks on how to self-publish within a year."

Laila Benzel
– Author and Inspirational speaker

"Grant was part of making our dream come true as he held our hands in releasing our book. It is, therefore, no surprise that this masterpiece was formulated highlighting the process, possible pitfalls, and ultimate sales success you will experience when you apply these well-researched principles."

Mandy Petrus
– Purpose Coach and Author of "Believe Again, A
Journey of Hope"

"The Golden Goose becomes an Authorpreneur is a practical and powerful call to action for aspiring authors. A recurring theme in the book is that the reader is the priority - a good example being this book. Put your seatbelt on and prepare yourself for a value-exchange ride."

Nondumiso Thango
– Speaker and Founder of Ada

"Pragmatic, expansive, and practical! 35,000-word golden key and a must-read for anyone who wishes to publish their own book. A guide that transforms your writing into a state of Flow."

Michael Ngarachu
– Investment Banker

"Imagine holding the first hard copy version of your own book; imagine introducing yourself as published author; imagine being able to hear the stories of how your book is impacting people's lives. This book will help take your imagination and make it a reality."

Seth Mulli
– Executive Director of the Youth Bridge Trust

"There is a phrase which states, 'the reason people don't start is because they do not know how to'. Thanks to this book, not only do I know how to start but also how to finish."

Tafadzwa Makombe CA (SA)
– Life Coach

"Grant Senzani is the inspiration that many aspiring authors need, particularly because he authentically shares his experience. He is know-ledgeable, honest, understanding, and vulnerable, which makes it easier to embrace lessons learned and shared.

The book cover is professional and appealing to its target market/audience. The book shouts "pick me!" as it stands out due to its calm yet daring colors and intriguing design.

The Golden Goose Becomes an Authorpreneur is comprehensive and an inspiring page-turner that provides enriching tools to write and publish a book. It compels you to explore your life journey by being self-aware while it serves as your guardian angel step-by-step. This "living" book is for keeps and reading it will translate to you taking action.

This book will help you realize, maximizes, and navigate your potential to writing your book. It is about informing, impacting, and influencing many lives to be lived meaningfully and for each person to live according to their purpose. It makes you realize that you cannot be the hiding shining light, but you must let your light shine. I immersed myself in the content of this book and I have been transformed mentally.

Mmatshepo Rebecca Sibiya
– Founder of Extraordinaire Ripples, Performance and Leadership Coach, Certified Facilitator, and Public Speaker/Master of Ceremonies

"One of the points that really stood out for me was where you say that we shouldn't wait for perfection before we complete any task, but rather get it done regardless and go back for correction. I for one, have sometimes struggled with the completion of tasks. The downside to that is that I almost don't complete my tasks."

Angela Casara
– Entrepreneur and Business Owner

"Grant offers a pragmatic yet inspirational blueprint on writing a book efficiently and publishing it profitably. I wish I had this guide before I wrote my first book. However, all is not lost as I will incorporate his lessons in my upcoming books."

Ntsundeni Ndou
– Author of 'Today is to Do' and Southern African Humorous Speech Champion

"Writing and publishing a book that pays can be a harrowing experience and a lonely road. The great news is that you have a friend and mentor in

Grant Senzani, who lays out a roadmap with practical stories and exercises that will take you from zero to Authorpreneur. If you want a way to get your message out there, add value to many people then this is a book that will help you get there. Get your mind and study materials ready, and in the end, be sure to thank Grant for the service to the world he is providing."

Njabulo James,
–Author of 'Inspired Success' and 'You Are A Business', and Distinguished Toastmaster

"It gives you mind-blowing advice on how to be an expert by becoming an author. The Golden Thread is explained and why it's important."

Tebogo Majokana
– Entrepreneur and Business Owner

"I love the conversational manner in which the depth of information in this book is delivered. Reading it feels like having a coach walk with me step by step in the journey of writing a book, making it the perfect go-to guide! The author is able to offer services that the emerging author will need as well as referencing his own journey, which gives this read an authenticity that says, "my becoming an author is possible, it is within my reach after all."

Divinity Roji
– Poet, Author, Speaker, and Entrepreneur

"I thoroughly enjoyed the conversational nature in which you take the reader through a step-by-step approach to getting published. The instructive nature of the book allows the reader to apply the various techniques that you suggest without being prescriptive."

Johnny Alubu Selemani
– Operations Director of Inyanda Capital

This book is the most informative, uncomplicated and humorous, yet extraordinary guide, to assist upcoming authors, to realize their dream of becoming an Author. I applaud the way the

The Golden Goose Becomes an Authorpreneur, is a necessary toolbox for every author with an entrepreneurial mindset for success. It is the most recommended step-by-step guide for those who are determined to propel from their humble beginnings of writing to creating multiple streams of income after publishing. Hats off to you Grant, for granting us the opportunity to be practical in the digging into our craft."

Divine Y. Keren
– Author of 'Above & Beyond', Poet, and Humanitarian

"It is literally a step-by-step fool proof recipe for moving one's author ambitions from aspiring to accomplished, complete with timelines and a virtual vision board right at the beginning. If you're not published after reading this book, then maybe you must admit you didn't read the book."

Lerato Rikhotso
– Aspiring Author

"If you are writing a book, want to write a book or are even just thinking about it - you have to read *The Golden Goose Becomes an Authorpreneur*. This book holds your hand through the entire process from conception to success. Yes, the journey to Authopreneurship may seem daunting - this book makes it less so. Believe in your dream, get this book, do the work!"

Mutali Nemadzivhanani
- Life Coach, Speaker, Storyteller, and Soon-to-be Author.

ADDITIONAL MATERIAL

I am not too sure about you but I grew up in the error where DVDs were popular. Our family would get one DVD on a Saturday evening and we would sit around the TV and watch it together.

The movies were really cool and I enjoyed the time we all would spend as a family.

Most DVDs came with an interactive menu. What came to intrigue me about these menus was the fact that they had cut scenes. These were scenes the director left out of the movie they created. These scenes for me would show how things may have ended differently for certain characters.

While sometimes I would agree to the material and sometimes, I would frown at it, I enjoyed the fact that it was there.

You have come to the end of this book and I have some material for you. Material I was not able to add otherwise I would have spent another year putting this book together.

You can find the material here:

https://drive.google.com/
open?id=1IbuvWm7_AuovawZj_
R3vPPPE15_Ali5b

At that link you will see what I call the author foundational matrix. It is an excel spreadsheet. On the first tab will be the Golden Thread and what a book is meant to encompass from the front cover all the way to the back cover.

The second tab is the reviewer's list. This is where you will put all the reviewers you would like for your book. It will also keep you accountable to send them reminders.

The third tab is about the prospect list. This list will consist of the people that you would like to attend your book launch or people you would like to sell your book to. This list is how any business starts traditionally - through your contacts and their networks. The more you have the better.

The fourth tab is goal setting, which I am sure you will get instantly. The purpose of that tab is just to keep you accountable.

Lastly, I also have PDFs that I use at all our company's self-publishing workshops.

I will from time to time add things and when you access the link, I am certain you will get that notification too.

If you would like any clarity on any of the material, please feel free to contact me at info@thegoldengooseinstitute.com